ALL LIVES
MATTER

Natasha,
  Continue on your path
of embracing life with
gusto! Love, Kelley

ALL LIVES
MATTER

05·06·21

KELLEY MANGES

"God Saved Me to Serve"

My Dearest Eric,

You will always be my favorite person to spend time with because it is with you that I enjoy the best and most stimulating conversations. Your intellect, sense of humor and your heart for those who are less fortunate have made you a stand-out guy.

I remember one winter evening when the two of us were sitting by the fireplace chatting. You said, "Mom, I like the fire because it's really cozy and it keeps us warm but being warm makes me feel sorry for the homeless people who are outside and cold right now."

My son, you are always willing to lend a hand; whether in a homeless shelter, while supporting those in the community who are mentally ill, disabled, HIV positive, justice involved or (in our home) in foster care. Despite your own circumstances at any given time, you always have enough love, acceptance, understanding and empathy to give to those who Mother Teresa refers to as untouchable.

In the past, you were always so giving with your foster brothers and sisters. On a couple of occasions, to make things work, you even agreed to give up your bedroom without giving it a second thought. When I felt the need to apologize to you as an adult for interrupting what could have been "your only child life," you said, "Mom, I loved having siblings [through foster care and adoption]. The saddest part for me was having to say goodbye when they left."

This book is dedicated to you because you have lived your life… and continue to live life as a testament to the title that ALL LIVES MATTER. I am always proud of you!

-Love,
Mom

ACKNOWLEDGEMENTS

I would like to thank God for all the love, joy and peace in my life and for allowing me to carry His love letter to the world. I would like to thank my Mom who always responded to me as if I were her eighth wonder of the world.

Many thanks to my best friend (my BFF), Dr. Rhoda Smith for being the "wind beneath my wings" and for always encouraging me to reach higher, stand taller and be kinder. Your continued support has helped me through this journey.

I would also like to thank my friend, my publisher and author of "Beauty for Ashes," Brenda D. Taylor. I appreciate the huge amount of encouragement you have always given me. I especially appreciate your love and encouragement on this long-awaited accomplishment of becoming a first-time author. You are the consummate role model and a wonderful friend.

Thank you, author and friend Michelle Larks, for putting up with my relentless questions about how you got from page one to page one-hundred, two-hundred, or three hundred while authoring your books. Your love, patience and support has helped plant the seed for *All Lives Matter*.

To my friend Terry Watson, the crème de la crème of public speakers. When I shared with you that I wanted to write a book, you handed me what looked like a bucket full of encouragement. Thanks so much of that, and thanks for being born in my lifetime.

Carlo Carma, I would like to thank you for saying yes to the first edit of my book. I have always been impressed with your skills as a journalist, as an editor and an all-around great guy. I am happy to be able to call you my friend.

Proverbs 19:20 tells us to, "Seek wise counsel." After being stuck and unable to move forward with *All Lives Matter*, I was blessed to be on vacation in Aruba with five women who impacted my life. They gave me the inspiration to move forward on this project. I lovingly refer to them as the Aruba posse: Dr. Rhoda Smith, Assistant Professor at Springfield College; Julie McKelphin, Non-Profit Management, Reiki Master and Certified Hypnotherapist; Deborah Holmes, Attorney at Law (retired); Denise Davison, more affectionately known as Dr. D, Assistant Professor at Morgan State University; Carol Joseph, Manager; Cathy Royal, Attorney at Law. Your wise counsel was instrumental in moving the manuscript out of my hands and into the hands of the publisher. I am forever grateful.

I would also like to thank the people who are the reason I've been able to walk through the figurative fire (repeatedly) without being burned; I am and will be forever grateful for the support from these lifetime friends and loved ones. Thank you, Carla Erickson, for your unwavering love and support "always" and in "all ways." Thank you, Jackie Anderson, for always being there, even when it meant dropping everything else just to rescue me. Pastor Andreton Jones and Dawn (Angel) Jones, thanks for working so effectively with God while selflessly helping me get back to a way out of no way on a countless number of occasions.

Thank you, Mary Fraser for always providing good times, great conversations and for a lasting friendship that means a great deal to me. I am also forever indebted to my friends Barbara Parker, Gary McConnell and the late Gary Handwerg for selflessly assisting me with my Bolingbrook Community Television shows. I am blessed by your everlasting friendship and love.

I am forever indebted to my sister and friend Gale Jones

for always reminding me that I am more than a conqueror and that no weapon formed against me shall prosper. Your continued and steadfast encouragement is priceless.

I'd like to give a shout out to all the people who have provided me with up to fifty-five years of friendship: Dr. Rhoda Smith, Denise Jordan, Julie McKelphin, Judie Gardner, Linda Wilson, Dr. Dawn Wynn, Fannie Cooper and the late Shelby McCline. My love for all of you is eternal. You have decorated my life with over five decades of love, joy, laughter, beautiful times and wonderful memories. Each one of you (at various times) has been my bridge over troubled water. I thank you. I love you and I can't wait to make fifty more years of memories with you.

Finally, I would like to thank my readers. The fact that you have *All Lives Matter* in your hands right now or are listening to it as you move to and fro, means the world to me. And in the words of six-year-old Alabama superhero Austin Perine, who delivers meals to the homeless in his community, "Don't forget to show love [to everyone] no matter what they look like."

Much love to you all.

TABLE OF CONTENTS

FOREWORD

While speaking to a group of master's level social workers at Springfield College about my book, one of the students asked how I could reconcile using the title "All Lives Matter" when so many people believe the saying disrupts the "Black Lives Matter" message.

My answer went something like this: I have been Black for over half a century. My motivation for writing this book was inspired by feelings of being sick and tired of the racial injustice in this country. The book was started before the "Black Lives Matter" movement and although several people suggested that I consider changing the title, I refused to loosen the hold on my experience, which translates to All Lives Matter.

When I worked as a co-facilitator with men who were court ordered to attend domestic violence classes, we had sessions that I called empathy walks. The purpose of the empathy walk was to remind the client that when their partner disagreed with them, it was not the time to lose their cool or blow their top. Instead, I encouraged them to ask questions, be respectful and empathetic, and dig deeper to find out why both parties felt the way they did.

Empathizing is not only a problem for men who are trying to recover in court ordered domestic violence classes. Our public is also struggling with extending respect, empathy, and forgiveness to our neighbor. While we are learning to love people, who do not look like us, love like us or worship like us, we also must work on empathizing with individuals who do not share our opinions.

"In order to empathize with someone's experience you must be willing to believe them as they see it and not how you imagine their experience to be."
Brene' Brown

This book is what I bring to the table because of my experience. I have worked with, volunteered with, and lived with people from all walks of life. I have been a volunteer with the homeless, in juvenile detention, in adult detention, with deaf and deaf/blind individuals, people who are HIV positive, those who are mentally ill, developmentally disabled, and autistic because Black lives matter.

I have worked with seniors, as a hospice volunteer, with women who are victims of domestic violence; and with men who perpetrate domestic violence because Black lives matter.

I have volunteered and worked with people who have substance use disorders because Black lives matter. I have parented the children of other Black families while doing foster care for children and teens because Black lives matter.

During my tour of duty as a foster parent I lived with teenage gang members and one teen youth who had been charged as a pedophile because Black lives matter.

The Bible tells me that God is love and as a result I surmise that He is also a God of inclusion. For me this translates to the fact that All Lives Matter and Black Lives Matter too.

LOVE YOUR NEIGHBOR
Who does not look like you
Think like you
Love like you
Speak like you
Pray like you
Vote like you
Love your neighbor
Even the ones who "don't" like you
No exceptions
Because ALL LIVES MATTER

Mere Image (Adapted)

All Lives Matter

In Western society we have our own untouchables. By our own behavior we demonstrate that certain people are not to be touched. The categories differ from individual to individual. For some it is prostitutes; for others it is people who are LGBTQ. Some dread those commonly referred to as "street people." Others avoid those who are justice involved, the mentally ill, those who are physically disabled, those who have been in foster care or even those who are dying.

"The love of God cuts across all those man-made barriers. And those who are truly in love with Him will be his agents for touching the untouchables." Mother Teresa fulfilled her call to love those who were considered untouchable. She got a call from God to be a Missionary of Charity in India, to become a carrier of love to those who felt unloved, uncared for, untouchable and unwanted.

In one of her famous quotes she said, "If you judge people, you have no time to love them."

There are some things that for me personally are hard to understand: Things I could confess to being ignorant about when it comes to the "why" of it. I do not understand hunters, hoarders and thieves. That does not mean that I am not on a mission to establish a better understanding of these issues. And... it does not mean that I feel any indifference toward the people who are involved in these behaviors.

My best friend, who has her PhD in social work, is my information source when I need questions answered about issues of humanity. She once tried to explain the etiology of the thief and I must admit I still do not get it. I have fostered teens in the past. A couple of my foster kids had problems with stealing. I did not blame them because I know that some behaviors are a result of all kinds of trauma, inclusive of being moved from home to home while in foster care.

My friend, who spent several years in child welfare before becoming a social work professor, told me that when a child in foster care has problems with stealing, it can be a result of issues with insecurity. I'll admit that even today I still find it difficult to intellectualize this point, but I have found that the more educated I am regarding the subject, the more empathetic I become.

My dear friend also explained to me that hoarders accumulate things to have control over their lives. Initially I was confused by this rationale as well but after taking a hard look at my own life, and examining some of my past behaviors, this idea began to make more sense to me.

There were times BC, before children, when I would decide not to clean the kitchen, not to make my bed or even clean the hair off the floor of the shower. I remember the day a good friend of mine stopped by unexpectedly and after looking around said, "Are you depressed?"

I was tickled and she had to laugh when she said it. Through our laughter, I told her that sometimes I let things get that way when no one was looking. Looking back now, I realize that at the time, my not so pristine apartment gave me a sense of being in control.

For hoarders however, this is a lot more complicated. I bring up my ignorance on the subject not to judge people who hoard, but to point out that we should try to educate ourselves on the things we do not understand.

As for hunters, well... unless you are killing for your food, I struggle to understand the sport. My son once tried to explain that there are times when an animal is multiplying so fast that there is not enough food for them to eat. His question to me was, "Mom, would you rather have them starve slowly or meet a demise that is faster and more humane."

I know more about hunting today than I did 10 years ago and although I am still not ready to join anyone on a hunting trip, I'm open to learning as much about the sport as I can. I am also willing to listen to anyone who would like to share their feelings with me on why they think it is an enjoyable sport. I would be willing to even hang out with hunters but only in the same way I spend time with skiers; by hanging out in the cabin and waiting for them to return for social time.

How can we all become more tolerant? What would it take for us to be willing to educate ourselves about the things and/or people we do not understand? Do the lives of the hunter, the hoarder, and the thief matter? Do the lives of those we deem untouchable matter? I stand by Mother Teresa's quote, "When we judge people, we have no time to love them." Despite our differences, we can make our world a better place by continuing to embrace the idea that all lives matter.

Black Lives Matter

*"This nation in which we were born is just one model of reality.
Other cultures are not failed attempts at being us. They are
unique manifestations of the human spirit. So, despite the
ugliness, despite the racism, let us continue to be one nation...
under God, indivisible,
with liberty and justice for all."*
-Author unknown; adapted

Black lives do in fact matter. As a Black woman, my own life is intertwined in this very statement. However, I would like to go a step further and argue the point that all lives matter. The lives of Black people; white people, those in the LGBTQ (Lesbian, Bisexual, Gay and Transgender, Queer) community, the disabled, the Christian, the atheist, and the Buddhist, those who are justice involved, the immigrant, the homeless person and everyone else we deem to be different or untouchable. This even includes hate groups like the Ku Klux Klan (KKK), Aryan Nations or Proud Boys, because when we are prejudice against those who are prejudice against us, we are trying to have two wrongs make a right and that never works.

Francis Bellamy, a Christian Socialist, wrote the pledge of Allegiance in 1892 for the September 8th issue of the *Youth's Companion*, which today would be equivalent to the *Reader's Digest*. I have been reciting this pledge for as long as I can remember, so when an associate asked, "Why do these people (meaning immigrants) keep coming over here (meaning to the United States) and taking over, I did not hesitate in my response. I said, "Because we are one nation, under God, indivisible, with liberty and justice for all."

Francis Bellamy, on the other hand, took *this* stand on immigration when he wrote the Pledge of Allegiance:

"Where all classes of society merge insensibly into one another, every alien immigrant of inferior race may bring corruption to the stock. There are races more or less akin to our own [which] we may admit freely and get nothing but advantages by the infusion of their wholesome blood. But there are other races, which we cannot assimilate without lowering our racial standard, which should be as sacred to us as the sanctity of our homes."

On the Teaching Tolerance website, a project of the Southern Poverty Law Center (SPLC), there is a statement:

"Somewhere in America
Every hour
Someone commits a hate crime.
Every day
At least eight Blacks, three Whites, three gays, three Jews and one Latino become hate crime victims.
Every week a cross is burned."

"Hate in America is dreadful, daily and constant: the dragging of a Black man in Jasper, Texas, the crucifixion of a gay man in Laramie, Wyoming," Post 9/11 hate crimes against hundreds of Arab-Americans, Muslim Americans and Sikhs are not isolated incidents. They are eruptions of a nation's intolerance," (SPLC).

Further eruptions of our nation's intolerance include a choke hold that precipitated the death of Eric Garner by police officer Daniel Pantaleo; an 8 minute 'knee on the neck' of George Floyd by officer Derek Chauvin that led to his death. Garner and Floyd's words, "I can't breathe" were ignored by officers in both cases. The shooting death of Walter Scott by ex-cop Michael Slager.

"Bias is a human condition and American history is rife with prejudice against groups and individuals because of their race, religion, disability, sexual orientation or other differences. The 20th century saw major progress in outlawing discrimination, and most Americans today support integrated schools and neighborhoods. But stereotypes and unequal treatment persist [creating] an atmosphere often exploited by hate groups.

When bias motivates an unlawful act, it is considered a hate crime. Race and religion inspire most hate crimes but hate crimes today wear many faces. Bias incidents (eruptions of hate where no crime is committed) also tear communities apart—and threaten to escalate into actual crimes." Teaching Tolerance

According to FBI statistics found on ucr.fbi.org, *in 2016 15,254 law enforcement agencies participated in the Hate Crimes Statistics Program. A few of the findings from the 6,063 single-bias incidents are as follows*:

- 57.5 percent were motivated by a race, ethnicity, or ancestral bias.

- 21.0 percent were prompted by religious bias.
- 17.7 percent resulted from sexual orientation bias.
- 2.0 percent were motivated by gender identity bias.
- 0.5 percent (31 incidents) were motivated by gender bias.

In his book, "What's Race Got to Do With It," Larry Elder calls for an end to "bitching, moaning and whining," and this is a reference made toward the African American community. On the one hand, I can support this premise when it leads people to use racism as an excuse for living a mediocre existence. On the other hand, racism hurts. It hurts individuals, it hurts communities, and it hurts African Americans.

I could stop moaning and groaning about the spirit of racism in this country if it were not for the fact that, even today, I continue to witness situations that are beyond blatantly racist.

Do any of these situations determine what is in store as far as my personal destiny is concerned? No, they do not. That's because I had a mother who single-handedly made me feel like I was in fact the eighth wonder of her world. The result of that love translated into this: If you knock me down (figuratively), like the pop-up dolls of old, I will continue to bounce right back up.

My youngest son and I used to bike together regularly when he was an adolescent. Usually when he approached a hill while riding, he would accelerate and take the hill with a vengeance. His attitude at the time was, "When the going gets tough, it's time to get tougher." I want him to always approach life that way. I want all my kids to embrace the attitude that if you are knocked down seven times, you get up eight. I want people who face racism, bias and prejudice to embrace this stance as well.

Religions Other Than Our Own Matter

There are children who are raised hearing, "Things will be different when you get to Heaven." They are given the vision that Heaven will be a sort of paradise with love abounding, a place that embodies an atmosphere of tolerance of religions, culture, and sexual orientation. So why worry about things that are happening here on earth?

This revelation may beg the question… "How can we emulate the essence of Heaven here and move to a place where there are no untouchables, where we have learned to really "love our neighbor" and where we truly believe that all lives matter?"

Sometime ago I visited the Universalist Unitarian Church of Joliet (UUC), which celebrated its 180th anniversary in 2016. During my visit there, I was moved to believe that this church could be on the right path to finding the answer. It is described by its parishioners as a form of Heaven in the here and now. The church embraces all religious faiths, as well as non-religious beliefs such as atheism, agnosticism and paganism. It is also a welcoming place for LGBTQ individuals.

At the Universalist Unitarian Church in Joliet, members believe they are promoting love and peace through diversity. However, outsiders have accused the organization of being like a cult.

The Universalists, who organized in 1793, and the Unitarians, who organized in 1825, merged in 1961 to become the Universalist Unitarian Association (UUA), which is made up of more than 1,000 congregations. According to Marta Flanagan, co-minister of the Universalist Unitarian Church of Portsmouth, NH, Universalist Unitarian is a liberal religion born on both Jewish and Christian traditions.

Gary Nolen, a long-time member of the UUC, says the church accepts people, no matter their beliefs. "It doesn't matter if you're Jewish, Catholic, Methodist, Baptist or Buddhist," he said. "This church is unique in its love, camaraderie and acceptance. I feel compatible with the church because I can love everybody."

The Universalist Unitarian Church covenant is a testament to that premise:

> *"Love is the doctrine of this church.*
> *The quest of truth is its sacrament.*
> *And service is its prayer*
> *To dwell together in peace,*
> *To seek knowledge in freedom,*
> *To serve humanity in fellowship.*
> *To the end that all souls shall grow*
> *in harmony with the Divine.*
> *Thus, do we covenant with each other and with God."*

Warren Thom, who has been a member of the church for 37 years and considers himself a spiritual atheist, says he is not put off by the reference to God in the church covenant. However, he points out that when he and his wife recite the covenant at Sunday service, neither of them recites the last word, which is God.

"We're not comfortable with [saying] that. With all our differences [in the church] the goal is to just be respectful," said Thom.

Sandy Costa is an ordained minister and a member of the UUC. She serves on the Board of Trustees and is actively involved with the pagan group at the church. Pagans are people who do not believe in monotheistic religions such as Judaism, Islam or Christianity. Costa says she feels that the other members of the church are very respectful of the Pagan group.

Gary Magruder has been involved with the church for 30 years. He has been with his partner for 47 years. "People are charged to be on an individual search for meaning in their lives. For some people it is spiritual and for some it is humanitarian. Most of my reason [for being here] is for the intellectual stimulation and the concern for social justice," says Magruder. "Being gay you become concerned with those who are in the 'other' category."

Addressing the assumption that the UUC is a cult, Margaret Jaraco, church treasurer, says, "If you mean a cult as a group that is secretive and won't let you go once you're in their clutches, and you're brainwashed into believing what they want you to believe, my response would be, no way!"

"This is the only group of people I've ever been around that patiently and respectfully listen to what I have to say regarding God and faith. This congregation lets me find my own way in my own time while always being available for discussion," said Jaraco.

Paul Cox, a human services worker who describes himself as a friend of the church for seven years, agrees with Jaraco's sentiment. "The sense of not having to conform to one ironclad creed is the most refreshing thing about this church."

What would happen if people allowed us to find our own way, in our own time? What if we made ourselves available to discuss our differences and even if we are conforming to ironclad creeds, we remained open and respectful regarding someone else's beliefs? What if this became our metaphor for life?

Is this what Heaven on earth would look like? Is there really any uncomplicated way to convince people that love is inclusive and that the lives of every individual on the planet matters? We could start by taking lessons from the Universalist Universal Church whose inclusivity is a roadmap to embracing differences and celebrating diversity.

In an article by Rich Nation entitled, "What's So Great About an Ethnically Diverse Church?" He said, "The Gospel is the true universal message. It applies to people who were adored by their parents and to people who were abused by their parents; bankers and the bankrupt; high school valedictorians and high school dropouts; the able bodied and the disabled; doctors and patients; jailers and prisoners; Black people, Whites, Hispanics, Asians, Native Americans—all are welcomed into God's kingdom without regard to language, performance, race, national origin or any other human characteristic."

I would add that for those who disagree with Nation and believe that they are the only ones who qualify to be welcomed into the Kingdom, those individuals could be met with this response:
"But He will reply, 'I don't know you or where you come from. Get away from me...'" (Luke 13:27)

Jewish Lives Matter

Jewish Tradition (from Deuteronomy 10:17) "For the Lord your G-d is G-d supreme and Lord supreme, the great, the mighty, and the awesome G-d, who shows no favor and takes no bribe, but upholds the cause of the fatherless and the widow, and befriends the stranger, providing him with food and clothing. You too must befriend the stranger, for you were strangers in the land of Egypt."

On June 11, 2009, James von Brunn, who carried a lifetime of hatred and a rifle to the entrance of the U.S. Holocaust Museum in Washington D.C., walked into the building with dark intentions. He was met at the door by a simple act of kindness–a security guard opening the door for him. Mr. Brunn fatally shot Steven T. Johns, the Black security guard who oversaw securing the Museum when Brunn entered.

According to interviews with family, friends, and civil rights groups, Brunn spent decades spewing hate toward Jews and Blacks—a hatred that was nearing a crescendo in the weeks before the shooting, (Nuckols, B., 2009).

During the same month, President Barack Obama toured the Buchenwald concentration camp in Germany, where he reminds us that, "tens of thousands of Jews perished during the Holocaust." These sights have not lost their horror with the passage of time. At the site Obama recalls seeing crematory ovens, barbed-wire fences, guard towers and a clock set at 3:25, marking the camp's liberation in the afternoon of April 11, 1945.

"Buchenwald teaches us that we must be ever vigilant about the spread of evil in our own time, that we must reject the false comfort that others' suffering is not our problem and commit ourselves to resisting those who would subjugate others to serve their own interests," Obama said.

My grandmother used to say, I can tell a person is a Jew from a mile away. What she was trying to imply is that she could tell a person was Jewish just by looking at them. The first time she said it, I was a teenager and even *I* was old enough to know better. I had heard her bias-based epithets before but this time I was thinking, "What is she talking about?

The last time I looked, Judaism was a religion and not a nationality. Even with that in mind, saying you know a Jewish person by looking at them would be comparable to saying, "I can look at a Black person and determine that they're Methodist or Baptist. It is ludicrous, to say the least. It was ludicrous then and still just as ludicrous today. Big exhale!

Unfortunately, when my grandmother made statements like these, I was unable to respond. If I ever tried to respond to any of her irrational thoughts, I would hear this: "Don't dispute my word!" In other words, disagreeing with her was never ever, an option. She had another famous line when either my sister or I would risk disagreeing with her and that was, "I'm your mother's mother!"

This is a little bit of a different subject, but I can't bear to pass up the opportunity to share. All my life I heard my grandmother pronounce the word children as "churen." One day, let's say it was the day I lost my mind. I said, mother dear, (which is what she was affectionately called), "the word is chil-dren, not churen."

Oh my gosh! I thought the top of her head was going to pop right off. She looked like her face was transforming in a hulk kind of way. When she finally recovered and was able to speak, she said, "Don't you ever correct me! I'm your mother's mother!!!" I can't say at the time that I was sure what she meant by this statement. But now...years later, I guess she meant she had been on the planet long enough to be all-knowing.

Although I loved my grandmother, she could be completely unreasonable and she did not like anyone who did not look like her, love like her, worship like her or think like her and that included people in the Jewish community. As much as she tried to influence me, I realize she was instrumental in my decision to live a different life.

Years later, a major life event led me to read the book, "When Bad Things Happen to Good People," by conservative Rabbi Harold S. Kushner. As I read the book, which I loved, I found myself stopping periodically to look at the cover. I was in my 20's and by this time I hadn't had any up close and firsthand experiences with the Jewish community.

I kept looking at the cover to be sure that a Jewish Rabbi authored the book because the book was beautiful, and I felt conflicted because of the negative press I had gotten from mother dear. I had been bamboozled into thinking that there was something bad about Jewish people, the Jewish community, etc.

Years later I worked part-time for a senior health care organization located in Northbrook, Illinois. The owners were Jewish and most of their clientele were Jewish as well. I worked with seniors in their homes who were more than happy to share information about their Jewish faith, culture, lifestyle, etc.

Because I am in the business of asking questions, I was able to get quite the education on the Jewish faith and the Jewish community. I celebrated Jewish holidays, learned a lot about services at the Jewish synagogue and even visited a couple of services myself.

One night, one of my clients spent over an hour explaining the difference in a Jewish funeral and a non-Jewish funeral service. The experiences were informative and life changing.

We have to let education, exposure and experience be our weapon against bias, prejudice, and racism. All lives matter, including the lives of every individual in the Jewish community.

Muslim Lives Matter

Muslim Tradition, from Surah 4:32:
"Do good unto your parents, and near of kin, and unto orphans,
and the needy, and the neighbor from among your own people, and
the neighbor who is a stranger, and the friend by your side, the
wayfarer and your servants."

"Christians and Muslims are brothers and sisters,
and we must act as such." -Pope Francis

In an article printed about Terry Jones, Pastor of the Dover World Outreach Center, the Gainesville, Florida minister is standing near a sign that reads, "A Mosque at Ground Zero Spits on the Graves of Those Who Died on 9/11." The sign is referring to those individuals who lost their lives when the twin towers in New York City were hit by hijacked planes on September 11, 2011.

For a time, Jones decided he would mark the anniversary of September 11th by burning the Quran to show his contempt for the idea of an Islamic Center being built at what can now be considered sacred ground.

After a visit from the FBI and several calls from high-ranking officials, including the President of the United States, Jones caved in. He decided it would not be a good idea to burn the book that Muslims believe is the word of God.

In an interview with Good Morning America, President Obama said what Jones proposed is completely contrary to our values as Americans. "This country has been built on the nation of freedom and religious tolerance," he said.

Gwen Austin, Independent Speaker and lecturer in Berkeley, California said, "We have other churches right here in America that teach things that are controversial and are the result of backwards thinking. One example would be teachings that encourage hatred for gay individuals."

"Since colonial times, Americans have used hatred as a common bond. Many groups target individuals with whom they do not identify for discrimination, violence, and neglect. When these groups formally organize themselves around the rally cry of hate, we consider them to be hate groups," Burton, C.E. et. al.

According to Austin, "Burning a sacred book does not solve anything, but instead points to everything that fuels hate and discrimination."

Hillary Ortiz, former graduate student at Lewis University, who is now a licensed clinical social worker (LCSW), believes Jones was using extreme tactics to reach a personal goal. Ortiz said by threatening to burn the Quran, Jones was inciting fear into the minds of American citizens.

"Why aren't his extreme Christian views seen as terrorism? It seems every Muslim [who walks down the street] is automatically labeled a terrorist, whether they are from Iraq, Afghanistan, China or Bosnia," says Ortiz.

Valerie Pinkston, clinical re-entry case manager at the Illinois Department of Corrections, says she didn't believe a mosque should be built near Ground Zero. Although she did feel that burning a holy text is the ultimate form of disrespect and should not be tolerated under any circumstances.

Pinkston goes on to say if the Qurans were burned, it would put American troops in danger and fuel the recruitment of extremist soldiers for Al Qaeda. She also added, "In my opinion, this Pastor did nothing more than act like a 2-year-old by stomping his feet until he got what he wanted."

I have volunteered in the past with Cook County Jail Ministry (CCJM). It is an initiative comprised of a conglomerate of individuals from different churches in the greater Chicagoland area. CCJM hosts a prayer breakfast three or four times a year. It is customary practice for volunteers to give a report on what is happening in each area of the jail. For example, one person will stand and talk about successes and concerns with Area One in the jail. Then another will pray for Area One, then on to Area Two and so on.

At one breakfast, the leader of the volunteer organization stood up and gave his presentation on Area Two. Now maybe it's just me, but sometimes I make assumptions for reasons that may only make sense to me.

Let us say for example… you are a white family and I see African Americans regularly coming to your house to visit. I might assume that you are a family that is open to differences, that diversity is a part of who you are.

If you happen to be married to someone whose race is different from your own, again I will assume that you are open to differences as well. If you grew up in a neighborhood surrounded by people who don't look like you, I might assume that you're even more open to differences and diversity.

For the same reason, if you go into jail or prison to minister to the inmates there, I will again assume that you are open to differences. However, we all know what they say about assuming. Yeah, that. But sometimes you can also miss the mark.

I must say I was taken aback when our fearless leader stood up and gave his presentation on Area Two. He mentioned how uncomfortable he felt during the time that he was volunteering in that area. He went on to explain that he felt uncomfortable because there were a few Muslims on the unit who were opposed to having a Christian minister come into the area.

Despite his understandably uncomfortable account of the situation, I was thrown off when he said, "Having to deal with the Muslims was like having Satan in the room with him." Really? Wow! Maybe it's just me… but don't Muslim lives matter? If you are a minister, which he was, you certainly know about 'welcoming the stranger.' I'm thinking… "there must be some way to make the meeting at the jail inclusive so that everyone in the room is comfortable, including him."

I understand that there is a lot of negative propaganda about Muslim conversion in U.S. prisons and abroad. I believe some of it. I believe if you take a person who is unstable to begin with and teach him or her some radical version of Islam, the results can be radical. However, on the other hand, Islam is the second largest of the three major monotheistic religions, the others being Christianity and Judaism."

There are five basic beliefs in Islam:
1. Belief in the oneness of God
2. Belief in the angels of God
3. Belief in the Books of God "These include the Quran (given to Muhammad), the Torah (given to Moses), the Gospel (given to Jesus), the Psalms given to David), and the Scrolls (given to Abraham)."
4. Belief in the Prophets
5. Belief in the day of judgement
6. Belief in the divine decree

The practice of Islam is based on "Five Pillars":
1. Shahada: To declare one's belief in God and the prophetic role of Muhammad.
2. Salah: To pray five times every day (dawn, noon, afternoon, sunset, and evening).
3. Zakat: To give charity to those in need.
4. Sawm: To fast from food, water, and other bodily pleasures during daylight hours in the month of Ramadan.
5. Hajj: To make a pilgrimage to Mecca at least once in a lifetime if it is physically and economically possible.

There are people who leave prison rehabilitated. Some of them leave the same way they came in but some of them leave as Christians. Some of them leave as Muslims and some of them leave without having practiced any religion at all. There is bad in all groups. I'm amazed at how easily individuals can write off an entire group of people because of the wrongdoings of a few.

There are people in all religions with mental health issues that might lead them to dysfunctional or dangerous behavior. However, there are millions of Muslims in this country and abroad who are upstanding non-violent citizens. There are also those in jail who have been able to change their lives because of the support of the Muslim community.

To say that having people in the room who have Islamic practices is akin to being in the room with Satan is unfair and not a clear picture of what Christianity stands for. Am I judging? If the shoe fits, I will wear it. I've about had it with people who elevate themselves to the point where they feel they can look down on others, especially when it's in the name of Christianity. All lives matter and God's love is inclusive.

The Buddhist
Life Matters

Thirty miles outside the city of Chicago, in the suburb of Lisle, is the Amitabha Buddhist Library of Chicago. Keeping in line with their effort to promote a harmonious environment, Director Li-Su L. Tan and her husband, Co-director Bert T. Tan provide a warm welcome for all their guests. Library volunteers help to prepare visitors for a morning session of meditation and chanting. A vegetarian lunch and a lunchtime Dharma talk are also included.

Umber Rahman, former President of Lewis University's South Asian Student Association, (SASA), at the time, said she sponsored the event to try and help individuals open up to the several types of cultures in the world. Rahman, who identifies as Muslim, sponsored similar events with SASA and the group also visited a Hindu temple. "I feel if people get to know each other better, they will have more appreciation for one another," she said.

For Ken Smith, now Director of Student Affairs, College of Pharmacy at the University of Illinois, the trip served as his second time visiting the library for the Buddhist ceremony. "My first visit was overwhelming because during the chanting ceremony we were joined by seven Buddhist monks who were visiting from different parts of the world," he said.

The Buddhist ceremony I attended was free from influential visitors, which gave participants an opportunity to relax while engaging in walking and sitting meditation. Chanting the phrase "NA MI TUO FUO" – which is derived from Amitabha Buddha – occurred simultaneously, while paying tribute to the Buddha by kneeling and bowing throughout the ceremony.

According to Li-Su, during chanting, the Buddhist hopes to become the same as the Amitabha Buddha. Bert explained that meditation is a practice of clearing one's mind. "There are thousands of thoughts running through your mind all the time. Whatever you do, always try to keep your mind in a tranquil condition," he said.

By clearing the mind, the Buddhist hopes to achieve nirvana. "Nirvana is a form of enlightenment: it is freedom from all worldly concerns such as hate greed and ignorance."

In his book, The Four Agreements, Don Miguel Ruiz states, "Humans punish themselves endlessly for not being what they believe they should be. We can presume that achieving nirvana will free people from punishment such as this as well."

Gerry Bouey, PhD, and Adjunct Faculty member at Lewis, who is a devout follower of Jesus Christ, said what he learned from the chanting and meditation session is that chanting reigns in the mind, and that following Buddha is more of an educational construct [than a religious one].

Regarding her meditation experience, Rahman said she felt like everything was cleared from her mind and that she was able to focus. "It was a cleansing experience. I can actually see myself using the chant in the future," she said.

"I believe you must think of chanting like you would exercise," said Bouey. "In order to benefit from it, you have to work at it. For example, if you are exercising to lose weight and you suddenly stop, you will no longer benefit from it and [probably] gain the weight back. Chanting is the same in that the more you do it, the more focused you become. If you stop doing it, you will lose your focus," he said.

After the morning chanting and meditation session, the library provided a vegetarian lunch that consisted of more than ten meat free dishes and fresh fruit. The Dhamma talk or Buddhist teachings followed with a story of the Infinite Life Sutra told by Li-Su. In the teachings she mentioned the Ten Virtuous Deeds.

These deeds are the roots for purifying the karma of the body, speech, and mind. Li-Su said if we control our speech and our body, our mind would be easy to control. She added that keeping the pitfalls of others in our mind is like garbage collection. "You must get rid of those thoughts," she said.

Yvonne Zambrano, a student and a member of the St. Nicolas Church in Chicago, said, "This experience was definitely different from what I'm used to, but I have a brand-new insight on a different religion. I felt totally at ease and recommend that other people try this experience."

Tidiany Diarra, A workshop specialist for Player Programs and a Muslim, said he attended the ceremony because he wanted to experience another religion. "It made me realize that there are other religions in the world that still believe in a higher power and have diverse ways to pray."

Smith felt that the visit to the library gave him a better understanding of the various parts of the ceremony. He also added, "The experience [for him] was enlightening and educational."

The Wiccan Faith

Hollywood created a huge interest in witches when they produced an inaccurate depiction on the popular television series, "Charmed." For some, the show made witchcraft appear alluring, inviting, fun and at times, even sexy. Christian critics were concerned that teenage girls would be influenced by its allure and drawn into the demonic clutches of what is commonly referred to as "the craft," witchcraft or Wicca.

Some Christians believe that participation in this Pagan religion will guarantee those involved a place in the "lake of fire."

"But the cowardly, unbelieving, abominable, murderers, sexually immoral, sorcerers, idolaters and all liars shall have their part in the lake which burns with fire and brimstone, which is the second death." (Revelations 21:8)

Despite the negative misconceptions that shroud the Wiccan belief, their main tenet is to do no harm. In Silver Ravenwolf's book, "Teen Witch: Wicca for a New Generation," he writes, Witchcraft is a nature based, life affirming religion that follows a moral code and seeks to build harmony among people and empower self and others." He describes Wicca as "...the art and science of white magic, a gentle, loving practice."

Contrary to widespread belief, Wiccans do not believe in hurting people, killing animals, telling lies, doing sexually pervasive acts, drinking animal's blood, stealing, summoning devils, (they don't believe in demons) or performing black magic. Wiccans do not believe in the devil and view him as only an element of the Christian religion.

Where Christians have the Ten Commandments, Wiccans have only one rule, which is to harm none. They have two other important tenets that ground their structure: To have perfect love and to have perfect trust.

Sandy Costa, an ordained minister, and follower of the Wiccan faith, says paganism, or the Wiccan philosophy has a lot of traditions that revolve around nature-based spirituality. According to Julie McPherson, who has been practicing paganism for the past 12 years, Wiccans have an appreciation for nature, support of women's rights, non-judgmental attitudes and an enticing offer of spiritual growth and self-improvement.

According to Costa, pagans do not proselytize or try to convert others to a religious faith or political doctrine. "We do not have a universal text and we see God as God and Goddess, which is our way of reclaiming the feminine face of the Divine. Further we do not see our deity as being punitive," said Costa.

"As Wiccans we practice magic," she said. "We consider our spell work to be more an act of meditation that involves placing our intention in the hand of the Divine. I also consider myself to be a witch which means that when I do spell work, I use the forces of natural objects in my practice."

"Our calendar is the wheel and as most people know, Halloween is our new year. We celebrate the New Year by honoring our ancestors and calling on them to visit with us," said Costa.

Other celebrations include the Esbats and Sabbats. Esbats involve the moon and its phases. The eight Sabbats are major celebrations for Wiccans. Modern pagan belief is the rule of three. Everything you put out into the world comes back to you three times. "With this rule in force, in paganism, no one would want evil to come back to them three times, therefore it is better to send positive energy into the universe," said McPherson.

"We are much like everyone else," said Costa. "Our values are the same, but our methods are different. Most of us are smart enough to know that none of us have all the answers."

One of my friends of over 50 years has been a Wiccan for most of our adult life. It hasn't had any effect on our friendship. I respect her choice and she respects mine. This friend babysat my dolls, for crying aloud, when we were only 8 years old. A friendship such as this one, that has sustained more than a half-century, is solid and cannot be changed by who or in what way we worship.

You might have guessed that I have had a few of my other friends raise an eyebrow or two when I let them know ahead of time that my Wiccan friend would be joining us for dinner or for another event. I do not know what they expected, but they were always surprised to find a loving, kind and caring individual who just happened to be drawn to a different faith. I agree with Costa. Most people who practice the Wiccan faith are much like everyone else.

The Catholic
Church Matters

When I was around eight years old and living in Chicago, I noticed activity on the corner of the block where I lived. Eventually it became apparent that a new house was being built. It was not a large house. It turned out to be a one-story ranch after all the work was done. However, in our south side neighborhood, the house stood out like a mansion.

It was brand new, and it didn't just look white, it was a color of white that stood in great contrast to all the other houses and apartment buildings in my neighborhood. It looked like a misplaced house in a fairy tale. It just sat there in the middle of what (we didn't know at the time) was our ghetto.

When the house was complete, my friends and I waited with curiosity and anticipation for the newcomers to arrive. It was not long before we saw a lot of white people milling in and out of the house and taking in furniture that didn't seem to be new. Who were these nice people? They didn't even yell when we stepped on their grass; grass that had been laid so perfectly around their home.

We learned later that the house belonged to one person, a Catholic Priest. This Catholic Priest, who I'll be referring to as Father Joy, arrived in our neighborhood with a mission in mind. He was the new leader of a Catholic Church that was just blocks away from our south side apartment, where I lived with my grandmother, my mother, and my sister.

Father Joy started several programs that were open to adults and children in our neighborhood. Although I can't remember his given name, I am sure I could find his picture in the dictionary under the word "saint." This priest was *all that* and a bag of chips as the young folks used to say.

By age six, I was familiar with the Catholic Church because I had attended kindergarten at a Catholic school. At that time, I also attended the church that was affiliated with that school.

This incredibly positive start with the Catholic Church shaped my feelings about a lot of things in life. Our neighborhood church kept us very busy and out of trouble. Father Joy made sure that he provided plenty of after school activities to decorate our lives.

He is the reason I became a girl scout and was able to attend the School of Human Dignity. With the help of a few parents in the neighborhood, including my mother, Father Joy started a few Girl Scout troops. I joined the one that was age appropriate for me at the time.

This priest was also responsible for my visits to the nearby convent that was just a few blocks from my home. The nuns would take me with them when they went door to door to pass out flyers with information about the church. I loved doing that. It gave me a sense of worth and a feeling of importance.

Each time I accompanied one of the nuns on a door-to-door excursion, she would take me back to the convent to have lunch with all the other nuns. They were all white, but I really do not think I noticed that at the time. All I knew was that I was surrounded by a group of women who were kind, loving and made me their center of attention.

It made me feel like the lunchroom in the convent had to be the most beautiful and peaceful place on the planet. They always spoke calmly, lovingly, and quietly, hardly above a whisper. To me, it was like heaven on earth.

What I didn't understand at the time, which was a revelation to me later, is that it was a really innovative idea for the nuns to take me along on those door-to-door walks. People in our neighborhood did not readily open their doors to strangers and especially not to white strangers. When you lived in an all-Black neighborhood during the 60's and white people came to the door, the adults in the house would usually panic.

The panic was even more pronounced if that person were a white man. My mother is turning over in her grave from embarrassment because I am disclosing this information. But at our house, my family would be scurrying around all over the place just trying to figure out what to do whenever a white person darkened our front door.

I would imagine the behavior I saw in the 60's was reminiscent of behavior that could have dated as far back as the 1860's. Slaves never knew what to expect when a white person arrived at the door of their home or cabin and in the 1960's the remnants of slavery still hung in the air.

It didn't happen often at our house but when it did, people were rushing around rapidly repeating in hushed voices, "There's a white man at the door."

"Has anybody seen him around here before?" Someone else might whisper.

Still whispering, someone else might say, "Don't open the door."

Then, "Open the door and see what he wants."

The last time our door was opened for a white man, he was selling insurance. We thought he was either a very brave man or he was having a heck of a time trying to sell that insurance.

During slavery it must have been terrifying for my ancestors when a white person showed up at the door of their quarters. I would be willing to assume that most of the time it meant trouble. I am not making light of what my ancestors had to go through. I am just amazed at how the intensity of the situation carried over into my young life in the 1960's.

When people say Black people just need to get over it, and I am still talking about the remnants of slavery, they have no idea, but that river runs very deep. The wounds have healed but some of the scars are still there. People should know that we want nothing more than simply to "get over it."

However, it's not just something I need to do, or that Black people need to do. It is something the world needs to do. Love thy neighbor, forget the color of an individual's skin; accept them as they are with a disability, a different religion, a different sexual orientation, etc., and just love the "content of their character." Love thy neighbor because out of these three things, faith, hope and love; the greatest of these is love.

I believe the priest and nuns who came into our neighborhood during the 60's to help us in our struggle for dignity, self-respect and courage, were intuitive enough to know that it wouldn't be a good idea to go door-to-door alone. It all worked out because I loved to go along for the walks. When people looked down and saw me, they always opened the door.

I am sure that at first there was the initial panic. Then, after the initial panic, the thought process went something like this: "White nun wearing a habit; little black girl standing next to her; the child could be lost and maybe they think she belongs here. Maybe I should open the door."

Once that door opened, the recruiting started. I guess I can consider myself responsible for getting half the women in our neighborhood to get involved with the Catholic Church. Father Joy and the nuns all gave me a positive feeling about white people while I was still an adolescent. The way they entered my world and wrapped me in their figurative warm embrace had quite a lasting effect on me.

At that time, it didn't matter who came into my life with negative press about white people. Father Joy and the nuns had made a positive impact on me. Still today, my loyalty to the Catholic Church is unwavering. It felt a little like Malcolm X's revelation in his pilgrimage to Mecca in the book, The Autobiography of Malcolm X as told by Alex Haley:

"The color-blindness of the Muslim world's religious society and the color-blindness of the Muslim world's human society: These two influences had each day been making a greater impact and an increasing persuasion against my previous way of thinking. Never have I witnessed such sincere hospitality and the overwhelming spirit of true brotherhood as is practiced by people of all colors and races here in the Ancient Holy Land, the home of Abraham, Muhammad, and all the other prophets of the Holy Scriptures. For the past week, I have been utterly speechless and spellbound by the graciousness I see displayed all around me by people of all colors."

Malcolm X had spent the better part of his life believing and professing that the white man was the devil. After his pilgrimage to Mecca, he returned a changed man. His experiences, his exposure to differences and the education he got from those experiences began to change him even before he returned to U.S. soil.

"I will never forget the dinner at the Azzam home. I quote my notebook again: I could not say in my mind that these were 'white' men. Why? The men acted as if they were brothers of mine, and the elder Dr. Azzam as if he were my father." Of Dr. Azzam, Malcolm X said, "I had no feeling of him being a white man." In retrospect, I had no feeling at all of the nuns or of Father Joy being white either.

I feel very strongly that it is possible to begin to combat intolerance and ignorance with experience, exposure, and education. I think we can all learn from one another. As strange as it may seem, you may encounter someone who seems intolerant and unloving because that person may not have had any experience with a person of another race, sexual orientation, or disability.

My mother and father were divorced when I was young. Growing up as a child, I lived in the house with my mother, sister, and maternal grandmother. I realize now as an adult that as an adolescent I never really got to know a lot about my grandmother's past. I knew she was born in Alabama but any more than that was a mystery to me.

I assumed that something very tragic must have happened in Alabama because my grandmother never talked about her past or her childhood and since she believed that "children should be seen and not heard," I never asked her.

There were a few things about my grandmother that stood out. She stood at five feet and no inches, was well over 200 pounds and was one of the best-dressed women I have ever known. She took immense pride in always keeping her nails freshly polished and people always complimented her on what beautiful hands she had.

She had a very unpleasant disposition; she didn't take crap off of anyone and she DID NOT like white people. I was clueless about my grandmother's disdain for white people. And there was no easy way to get a clear understanding of why because it was an unspoken rule that she was not to be questioned.

Some of my readers already get it. My grandmother was born in 1906 in Alabama. It was a very tough time in those days back in Alabama for her. She constantly reminded my sister and I that we should never trust white people. "Never!" she would say with emphasis.

Because of these rants I became further convinced that Father Joy and the nuns, who were so delightful and whose company I enjoyed so much, could not be white. There was just no way.

The Immigrant's Life Matters

L ewis University Center of Ministry provided students with an amazing opportunity while I attended classes there. We were able to participate in the "Stranger to Neighbor" training, an interfaith bridge building symposium that encourages students to "work together for immigrant justice." The founder and Executive Director, Eboo Patel, created the Interfaith Youth Core to have young people go out and change the world. His philosophy is built on religious pluralism and includes:

1. Respect for another person's religious identity.
2. Mutually inspiring relationships across religious boundaries.
3. And common action for the common good.

At a prayer breakfast in Chicago, Patel said, "Interfaith leaders will change conversations, launch projects and have a vision where interfaith cooperation is the norm."

David Fraccaro, the Stranger to Neighbor trainer and Executive Director of FaithAction International House in Greensboro, North Carolina, told students at Lewis that the United States is the most diverse country in the entire world, whether you are looking at it from a cultural, religious, or racial standpoint. "But diversity can have a positive or a negative impact," he said.

During the 1840's there was a political group called the "Know Nothing Movement." The name originated from the organization's code of silence. Whenever someone was asked what went on in the organization, the member was supposed to say, "I know nothing."

"The Know Nothing Movement worked hard to curb the immigration of Irish and German Catholics. They encouraged expressions of hatred through church burnings and mob attacks against priests and immigrants." (Toth, Crews and Burton, 2010)

Although there are laws today that criminalize such behaviors, the Interfaith Youth Core recognizes that we have a long way to go before we succeed at welcoming all strangers into this country. Some of the stories told by the group reinforced that reality.

One student shared a story about her parents and their reluctance to be patient with a Chinese friend because she knew very little English. This prompted Reverend Fraccaro to open up dialogue on the difficulty of learning a new language.

Eric Kingue, a former International Business Administration student from Cameroon, Africa, who is now a MSTC candidate and Account Manager, shared his experience: "I came to Lewis [University] one year ago from

Central Africa to study," said Kingue, "I still have a heavy accent because we speak mostly French in Cameroon. I also notice that Americans speak very fast," he said.

Kingue says he thinks Americans do lots of things fast. "Everyone is always rushing and running to work or school and no one ever retires here," he said. Kingue says the elders in Cameroon are not that way. They slow down and take it easy at retirement, which is the same thing he says he wants to be able to do.

Fraccaro encouraged students to become Youth Interfaith Leaders by speaking out or by telling their stories, taking action by setting goals, following up, and inspiring others by recruiting new leaders and transforming communities.

He called them to search their own faith and see what they are called to do. "There are more than 200 centers in the United States where immigrants are being detained," said Fraccaro. "One way to welcome the stranger is to go visit one," he told the students.

"As of November 2017, according to a Freedom of Information Act request filed by the nonprofit National Immigrant Justice Center, ICE operated 1,478 Adult detention centers, a number that doesn't include the CBP [Customs and Border Protection] facilities, which are all within 100 miles of the southern border." (www.businessinsider.com, 2019)

A Beating Heart Matters

I have a grandson or granddaughter that was never born. My son, who lives in California, contacted me to say that his girlfriend was pregnant. Although we all knew that it was not happening under the best of circumstances, I was beside myself with excitement. It was not that I didn't already have grandchildren because I do.

But the chances of this offspring ever getting married or having children was enigmatic. As age twenty-nine rolled around for him, the family wondered and speculated as to whether marriage or children would ever become a reality for this one.

When the news came, I was ecstatic. I could hardly contain myself. I told everyone I knew and anyone else that I didn't know who would listen. It had finally happened. In the words of the Sponge Bob song, "[It was] the best day ever."

I felt like the air was let out of me when, about a month later, I got the news that my son's girlfriend had had a miscarriage. It was devastating news, to say the least. I realized that for the couple of months that my grandchild existed as a fetus, its life had affected me in a major way.

Before the miscarriage, I had decided that there was no way I could have a grandchild come into the world who would live three thousand miles away and I could not hop on a plane to see him or her; or pick them up to bring him or her to my home for a visit with grandma.

And furthermore, there would be no way I would be able to say no when asked to help with important things that popped up in his or her life. I could not have one more grandchild moving around on the face of the earth with a grandmother who had not left a legacy or fulfilled her destiny.

That tiny little fetus affected my life in ways that were unimaginable. I was motivated to succeed at things and in ways I had never been motivated to succeed before. The spirit of this little one had propelled me forward like nothing ever had before. I wanted to finish projects, create new projects, and make my mark on the world.

By the time this child was born, I wanted to catapult into what would look like super grandma status. There is a quote from a book entitled *Destiny* by Tony Evans that had always had an impact on me but during the time my grandchild existed on this planet, encapsulated in the comfort of mom's womb of course, the quote came to life for me.

"To live without fulfilling your destiny is to be like the Dead Sea in Israel. It exists, but nothing can live in it. No fish can swim in it. Nothing can grow in it... Far too many people are living Dead Sea lives."

I no longer wanted to live a "dead sea life." I felt like I wanted to live out my favorite quote by Marianne Williamson:

"Our deepest fear is not that we are inadequate. Our deepest fear is that we are powerful beyond measure. It is our light, not our darkness that most frightens us. We ask ourselves, 'Who am I to be brilliant, gorgeous, talented, fabulous?' Actually, who are you not to be? You are a child of God. Your playing small does not serve the world.

There is nothing enlightened about shrinking so that other people won't feel insecure around you. We are all meant to shine, as children do. We were born to make manifest the glory of God that is within us. It's not just in some of us; it's in everyone.

And as we let our own light shine, we unconsciously give other people permission to do the same. As we are liberated from our own fear, our presence automatically liberates others."

That fetus, that beating heart that was three thousand miles away made me feel as if I had been born again mentally, emotionally, and spiritually.

I was ready to live out my life's purpose. I was ready to make manifest the glory of God that is within me—all because a child was near the point of being born, a child whose heart had touched mine in a figurative yet powerful way.

I gave birth for the first time when I was thirty years old. My first prenatal visit went something like this: The doctor asked, "How many pregnancies?" I responded by telling him that it was in fact my first. I was twenty-nine at the time. He then asked, "How many abortions and/or miscarriages?"

"None," I said, and the look on his face left me feeling fantastic. I thought to myself, "I wonder how many women come in this office and are able to say by age twenty-nine that they haven't had previous pregnancies. I do not mean to say that women should feel bad about being pregnant for the first time before they are almost thirty.

I do believe this is a fantastic opportunity to point out that I give Planned Parenthood all the credit. No matter what you think about Planned Parenthood, the organization has always been concerned about the unborn child. Planned Parenthood was instrumental in helping me get to my late twenties without getting pregnant. Let me explain.

When I was fifteen years old, one of my best friends got pregnant. She was fifteen as well. There was a group of about six of us who all hung out together. When the rest of us learned about the pregnancy we all panicked. Even those of us who were not sexually active felt like we needed to take some preventive precautions, just in case.

We all took a trip together to Planned Parenthood. I still thank God for the organization today. I would have never received the sex education I got from Planned Parenthood in my own household. While I was growing up, I never heard the word "sex" uttered by anyone in our entire household. As a result, until Planned Parenthood, my sex education lessons came from my teenage comrades alone.

At Planned Parenthood (PP), the education we received was nothing less than first class and top notch. Initially our visit with my closest friends included having us sit in a circle. There were a couple of healthcare professionals present to talk to us about sex, sexually transmitted diseases, pap smears, pregnancy, and anything else we had questions about.

My friends who were sexually active at the time were encouraged to have pap smears. The professionals explained how often we should have the procedure. We were also told that birth control was an option for anyone who was interested.

For those people who think that sex education (of any kind) encourages young women to run out and have sex or scarier still, become promiscuous; here are the stats on the lives of our group of six teenage girls several years later.

One of the six of us never had children; another teen in our circle started having children at age eighteen; another one of us started having children at age twenty-five; another at age twenty-seven and me at age twenty-nine. Friend number six was pregnant at age fifteen. Her pregnancy was pre Planned Parenthood.

Planned Parenthood does not get enough credit for preventing teenage and unwanted pregnancies. I do know that they were responsible for changing outcomes for me and my friends. That also includes other young women we encouraged to go to Planned Parenthood as well.

Like Planned Parenthood, I believe the life of the unborn child matters. I also believe if you can prevent an unwanted pregnancy in the first place, you are displaying foresight and careful consideration of what it means to be a parent.

I am not impressed by those people who use an exorbitant amount of energy to stand up against abortion. It is my opinion that they are not concerned about children but are more concerned about making some noise. What good does it do for the unborn child or the mother to have people standing outside of a place that performs abortions screaming and yelling and carrying signs? It is a waste of useful energy. Yeah, I said it and I stand by it.

I believe if you really want to be instrumental in making a difference, you should take in and provide care for the children who are already here, especially those who have been abused and neglected.

The Unborn Child Matters

I believe that the life of the unborn child matters. I also believe that people who spend time picketing, protesting, and praying outside of abortion clinics are well-meaning in their effort to make a difference.

I have seen videos of live abortions. They are heart wrenching and heart breaking to say the least. But I have also seen and heard horrendous stories of abuse and neglect; stories from children in foster care; stories from children in juvenile detention who have never had a family to call their own. I have read about horrific stories of abuse, one that included a young child being sodomized with a cow prod.

This year, there are more than 400,000 children (about half the population of Delaware) in foster care in the United States. The number of foster children up for adoption is a little over 100,000. "This means about 1 in 184 children in the United States are in the foster care system." Do not get me wrong. Just like my unborn grandchild that never made it into the world, his or her beating heart mattered.

But with such staggering statistics and with so many kids in foster care waiting for adoption, it just seems more feasible (in my opinion) to foster or adopt. Because the question becomes, while we are standing outside of the abortion clinic protesting, what are we doing for all the motherless and fatherless children who are already here?

I do understand that not all of us are able to foster or adopt. Having done both, I must admit that it is not easy. It is the kind of challenge that requires you to be strong to survive. But there are other things you can do for the children who are in the system. You can start by carrying a sign that reads, "Because a Beating Heart Matters, I Am Helping A child." I do believe if you're carrying the "Stop Abortion" sign and protesting outside of abortion clinics, a child's beating heart really does matter to you.

However, I would like to encourage you to focus that energy on at least one of the more than 400,000 children in our foster care system. Or...you could mentor a teenage girl and take her to Planned Parenthood to help prevent a pregnancy in the first place. You can volunteer; you can donate your time in juvenile detention, where some of our foster children end up.

You could be creative like the former foster child who decided that foster kids should not have to move from place to place with all their belongings in a plastic bag, so he decided to purchase more appropriate carriers for them.

I would like to share that story featured in People magazine and entitled, Former Foster Child Devotes His Life to Helping Thousands of Other Kids in Foster Care – One Backpack at a Time.

"When Rob Scheer opened his door in 2009 to meet his first-ever foster children, he did not expect to be reminded of an old, painful memory that would propel him into philanthropic action. But the jolted memory was so powerful that it eventually prompted Ro and his husband, Reece, to found a charity that has now helped more than 20,000 children. The Scheers' charity, Comfort Cases, provides foster children with backpacks filled with comforting supplies to carry with them as they traverse what insiders call "the system." The hand-packed bags replace the standard-issue foster child suitcase: A plastic trash bag.: (People.com, Susan Keating).

As has been pointed out, there are several ways to help children who are "in the system" that make a lot more sense than creating a ruckus outside of Planned Parenthood or abortion clinics.

Yes, the life of the unborn child matters. But we need to focus on making it matter more after the child is born than before. We must jump into the trenches and be a part of their permanency, be a part of filling their love tanks, be a part of making them feel wanted and helping them to live life to its full potential.

"When a child is born and they cry, the world should rejoice," but we can also rejoice over the results of making a difference in a child's entire life.

Practicing What I Preach

I would be remiss if I presented a book entitled, "All Lives Matter" along with my thoughts about tolerance (resulting from education, exposure, and experience), and not take the time myself to delve into another culture. It is important for us to reach outside of ourselves, even at the risk of being uncomfortable, to make the world a better place. It was as important for me as for anybody else.

I love the lyrics in Michael Jackson's song, "Heal the World." "Heal the world, make it a better place, for you and for me and the entire human race. There are people dying, if you care enough for the living, make it a better place for you and for me."

Or how about the song, "We Are One," produced by Maze featuring Frankie Beverly in 1983. "Can't understand why we treat each other in this way; taking up time with the silly, silly games we play. We have our love, and no matter how it's said or done... We are one. No matter what we do, we are One... Our love will see us through. We Are One."

I had to make more of a personal effort to step out and learn more about a group of people who are from a different culture or religion or sexual orientation, who don't look like me; who are disabled; who are dying, incarcerated, homeless or in foster care.

The first thing I did was sign up for a Spanish Meetup. Meetups were popular on the internet at the time and included a myriad of meetings of genres of all kinds. There are Meetups for runners, Meetups for singles, Meetups for dancers, etc.

At my first meeting, I sat through a three-hour presentation on nutrition that was presented entirely in Spanish. After the meeting was over, I met a Spanish instructor and immediately signed up for Ole Spanish School, where a person could become fluent in Spanish in as little as six months.

I realized that I would need to be immersed in the Spanish language and culture in ways other than spending time in class. I took a short break from my church and joined a church that has a service where Spanish and English are spoken. For a while, I attended Spanish school on Saturday and a Spanish church service on Sunday.

The Spanish Meetup

When I walked into the Spanish Meetup, everyone was speaking Spanish. No one was speaking English. All the people in the room were Hispanic. A few people said hello when I walked in, but those initial greetings were the only time I engaged in communication at the Meetup that day. I would, however, be involved in a lot of listening.

After about thirty minutes of sitting and listening to the Spanish speakers in the room having conversations amongst themselves, a very nicely dressed man took the floor. I was able to interpret at least about fifty percent of the presentation.

Later, I spoke to the Spanish teacher and he said I could start classes the following week. I told him I would be there. Most of the subsequent Meetups were scheduled in the evening on Saturday, which conflicted with my work schedule, but my goal was to find as many ways to engage and learn as much about Spanish culture as well.

I took the plunge to get you, my reader, to consider taking the plunge as well. I want to be a person who practices what I preach. They say the best way to learn about another culture is to learn the language. I have been saying for years that I wanted to learn Spanish. I took classes here and there. After I decided that I would be making suggestions to the rest of the world about buying into the principle that "all lives really do matter," I had to take a giant step to make a conscientious effort as well.

My Life Matters

It was way back when... In the days when I really was "knee high to a grasshopper," as the old folks used to say. We had relatives visiting at our home and this was one of those days—finally, when children got a chance to be seen and heard.

My maternal grandmother, like I mentioned earlier, used to always say, and I repeat, "Children should be seen and not heard," and she meant it. I am sure this was a prerequisite for the development of low self-esteem issues that followed some young people right into adulthood. The problem is when you hear this as a kid, you begin to believe you are not worthy of being heard.

I was in our living room sharing a story with my cousin about a bullying incident that occurred at school. My mom, who was in the kitchen minding her own business, stuck her head through the kitchen door into the living room. She was responding to something she thought she heard me say. She thought she overheard me say that I was part of a group of kids who were involved in humiliating and bullying a classmate.

My mother, who had a reputation for being soft-spoken and easygoing, moved in and corrected me with a swift reprimand. She said, in a strong tone that was very unlike any she ever used, "If I ever hear that you've been mean to anyone because they're different, my heart will break into a million pieces. It's wrong and I did not raise you that way."

My mother sat down and continued her diatribe, "and further, every person in this world is precious. When you see someone suffering at the hand of any group, I expect you to step up and do everything humanly possible to change the outcome."

My mother's reprimand reminded me of a quote by Bill Nunan, A Satellite Communications Engineer who says in the book, "This I Believe," *"Physics explains my body but not my soul. I believe my soul inspires me to make decisions to diminish pain and increase love in the lives I touch."*

My mother's message also inspired me to increase love in the lives of others, and I will never forget those words.

I had a similar feeling when my mother read the book, "The Hundred Dresses" to me. It was a book written in 1944 by Eleanor Estes about a young girl named Wanda Petronski. Wanda was teased at school because she was impoverished and had what seemed like an unusual last name. That book helped to shape who I am today. It had a powerful effect on how I respond to people who are different.

I can think of one more incident that had a tremendous effect on my life. It was when I saw the movie, "Of Mice and

Men." The movie was adapted from a novel written by John Steinbeck and published in 1937. It was about two brothers trying to make a living during the Great Depression.

One of the brothers was developmentally disabled and was provoked into what became a tragic end to the story. The developmentally disabled brother was tempted by a lonely and wicked woman to show physical affection toward her, but things got out of hand and he killed her. The men in the town hunted him down and killed him.

When the movie ended, I was inconsolable. I was only seven or eight years old at the time, but I could not control my tears. I could not stop thinking of how unfair it all seemed. I remember my mother's attempt to reassure me.

"It's only a movie," she said.

She went on to explain that the disabled man who was killed at the end of the movie was merely an actor who was only pretending to be dead. But even at the age of seven I already knew how cruel people could be (in real life). Yes. It was a movie. But it was an accurate depiction of what happens in life when people are fueled by hatred, ignorance, intolerance, and prejudgment.

These were the stories that helped shape my life and mold me into the person that I now share with the rest of the world; especially with those people society feels they have a right to judge: People who are HIV positive; alcoholics; drug abusers; sex offenders; gang members; LGBTQ individuals, foster children; people who do not look like us; worship like us; the un-churched; the disabled and even people who are dying.

One of my Sunday school teachers read the story of the Good Samaritan to me. After hearing that story, all I wanted was to be like the biblical Good Samaritan for the rest of my life. I vowed to do even more than model the "Good Samaritan," but to always stand up for people in real life who were like Wanda Petronski in the book, "The Hundred Dresses" and Lennie Small in the movie, "Of Mice and Men."

"And who is my neighbor?" In reply, Jesus said, 'A man was going down from Jerusalem to Jericho, when he was attacked by robbers. They stripped him of his clothes, beat him and went away, leaving him half dead. A priest happened to be going down the same road, and when he saw the man, he passed by on the other side. So, too, a Levite, when he came to a place and saw him, he took pity on him. He went to him and bandaged his wounds, pouring on oil and wine. Then he put the man on his own donkey, brought him to an inn and took care of him. The next day he took two denarii and gave them to the innkeeper. 'Look after him.' He said, and when I return, I will reimburse you for any extra expense you may have. Which of these three do you think was a neighbor to the man who fell into the hands of robbers?' The expert in the law replied. 'The one who had mercy on him,' Jesus told him, 'Go and do likewise'" (Luke 10:29-37)

When I decided to write this book, I not only wanted to make a strong point about how all lives matter, but I also had the crazy idea that I could help people at least contemplate coming back to having love for everyone, even those people Mother Teresa described as untouchable. I wanted to remind people that God IS love and that love is all encompassing.

Thoughts like these put me in the mind of a song by gospel singer Karen Clark Sheard entitled, "Authority." She prefaces the song with these words: God is not restricted to America. We serve a global God. We serve a universal God.

He is a God of every nation. He is an omnipresent God. He can be here and there and everywhere at the same time."

Whether we are God's ambassadors or not, we have the power to spread love globally, universally, here, there and everywhere. Yes. This is the message I wanted to convey but amid it all, I also learned some things about myself. I learned even more about love and how better to convey it to those closest to me.

Although it's a little hard to admit, I learned some ways that I am falling short when it comes to loving the people that are closest to me, I am glad that it's true that teaching can also be a form of learning.

In the interim I have learned that my life matters. I have had deep level love experiences with people from the cradle to the grave; loads of them. There have been times when I have failed in love with those closest to me. I loved them but not actively enough; I didn't give enough; I didn't connect enough, and I certainly did not engage in gift giving enough. I am not only learning but also practicing…

"love that is kind, love that does not envy or boost, love that does not dishonor others and is not self-seeking. Love that does not delight in evil but rejoices in truth. Love that should always protect, always trust, always hope and always persevere." Adapted (1 Corinthians 13:4-7 NIV)

I have learned that we can love up close or from a distance. If we want to show love, in the words of the Dalai Lama, we should always practice compassion, especially with those people who have had little education, experience or exposure to people who look different, worship different or see things different from the way we do.

I have to say I am on point when it comes to loving people who do not look like me, act like me or talk like me.

But before you label me arrogant, let me add that I occasionally miss the mark.

A recent example is when I pulled into a 7-Eleven to get gas. I was in a big hurry because I left home a little later than I should have. So, when I pulled up to the pump, I said to myself, "Okay, I left home late but I can still get to my destination on time if I just use my card, purchase a smaller amount of gas (to be able to finish quickly), and all will be well."

Things *did not* go as planned. When I looked at the gas pump, there was a written sign that read, "Please come in and pay with a credit or debit card." And as I looked around, I noticed that this sign was on every pump! Ugh! What!!? I was not happy. So now, everyone in my path is going to get the poker face.

I was not my regular smiley faced, kind self with the cashier. When I got back to the car, I had to remind myself that the world does not in fact revolve around me. I also reminded myself that our behavior toward others, (when it is negative), whether they look like us or not, has everything to do with arrogance, pride, and ego.

I came to realize a couple of things that day: For one I needed to take myself off the pedestal and regularly do a reevaluation of the woman in the mirror; and two, I needed to keep in mind, as my son told me one day, so as not to be too hard on myself, that enlightenment is a journey and not a destination.

He said, "Mom, just when you think you reached a place of enlightenment [and you have it all figured out] suddenly there's that trigger that can come out of nowhere and bam! You feel like you're right back to where you started."

"It's a journey and not a destination," he said.

The Neighbor

My neighbor's front door is ten feet away from mine on the second floor of my apartment building. I do not know her name because she avoids me. I see her and her little Toto-esque pooch that she is usually carrying in her arms. Whenever I see her leaving her apartment to take him or her outside, she moves very quickly and always in my opposite direction. This is her regular modus operandi until she and the pooch make it outside.

I have attempted to engage her in conversation on a few occasions, but she awkwardly and nervously rushes away, seeming to be anxious to leave my presence. If I happen to see or run into her when she is exiting her vehicle, (when I walk out of the apartment door), it is her habit to keep her head down. If I see her running in the grassy area with her dog on the side of the apartment building, she turns and faces the opposite direction the minute she sees me.

And if she happens to be walking into the building as I am getting out of my car, she extends her time outside until I am safely tucked away in my apartment; it's only then that I hear her footsteps in the hall moving toward her apartment door.

I saw her one day when I was entering the building with a person who was visiting me at the time. I mentioned the behavior to my friend. I said I thought her behavior was not only perplexing but also hurtful. My friend's response was, "You call her behavior perplexing? I call it racist."

My question then is this: Why would someone who is uncomfortable with people who are different move into an apartment complex that houses a multiplicity of different races? Her behavior led me to a few other conclusions: She is shy; she's rude; she is in fact a racist; she is a racist and a

KKK member; she has mental health issues that include paranoia; as my grandmother used to say, "she has no home training," or she doesn't believe that "all lives matter."

And if all lives matter, I am going to choose the first life that matters to be my own. When a person ignores me or refuses to acknowledge that I exist, that person is trying to tell me that my life does not matter. On the other hand, I should be thanking my neighbor for her rude and insensitive behavior.

Her intolerance towards me reminds me of how *not* to behave. Her intolerance towards me forces me to be more sensitive to the feelings of those around me. Her intolerance towards me forces me to be more aware when I see others being ignored, shunned, mistreated, or hurt.

My ex-husband, who is white, had never seen a black person, in real life, until he went to college outside of his hometown of Bremen, Indiana. During his time at Purdue University in West Lafayette, Indiana, he admits that he saw African Americans on campus but never interacted with anyone of color during his time at Purdue.

After graduating, he landed a job with Prudential Real Estate in downtown Chicago, which is where we met. According to him, this was the first time he had an opportunity to exchange words with a Black person.

The encounter finally made him realize that for years he had been bamboozled. He was in his twenties at the time and for more than twenty years he said he had gotten what he felt was negative and inaccurate information from the press and from his peers about Black people.

This was in the early 80's when his hometown of Bremen had a population of a little more than 3,500 residents. Twenty years later the population had grown to more than 4,500 residents and according to a 2010 census there were 85.6% White, 0.4% African, 0.2% Native American, 0.3%

Asian and 11.1% other races. As anyone can see, his hometown was not a lot of help when it came to being exposed to people who were different.

This brings me back to the fact that education is a huge part of the process of getting us to a better place in our tolerance walk. I do not just mean formal education. I mean taking the time to broaden your horizons, jumping out of that comfortable place and into a place of commitment. A commitment to make the world a better place by learning more about people and things we don't understand.

I repeat, I am not talking about formal education. I am talking about education that is a result of exposure and experiences with people we know absolutely nothing about.

The Parts Company

I once worked for a parts company in Elmhurst, Illinois. There were about 1,500 employees at the time that I was employed there. This number is an educated guess because the company was reluctant to give out numbers in an effort (I was told) to maintain a certain amount of privacy. This is a parts company that does business nationwide and has clients that include major hospitals, universities, and celebrities.

When I was there, the company's 1,500 or so employees included many upper management staff and only one of them was African American. I do remember that there was an African American in the Human Resources department. As I think back now, this was an effort to have it appear to incoming employees that there were equal opportunities at the company. However, the equal opportunity idea turned out to be nothing more than a façade.

I wondered for the brief time that I worked there how a Black person would be able to keep their self-esteem intact when they were working for a company that did not believe that Black people could hold management positions. It reminds me of the Teaching Tolerance article entitled, "Hidden Bias: A Primer, The Effects of Prejudice and Stereotypes."

It says, "Studies indicate that African American teenagers are aware they are stigmatized as being intellectually inferior and that they go to school bearing what psychologist Claude Steele has called a 'burden of suspicion.' Such a burden can affect their attitudes and achievement." Similarly, studies found that when college women are reminded their group is considered bad at math, their performance 'may fulfill this prophecy.'"

This is the same feeling one could get while working at the parts company in Elmhurst. When you have a huge number of employees working for you and none of the managers are Black, it is easy for your African American employees to feel stigmatized as being too intellectually inferior to hold the management position.

One day, I casually asked a coworker, who had been working for the company a lot longer, why there were not more African American managers. She responded by assuring me that there *were* more managers of color. They just happened to work at the Atlanta branch of the facility.

That is simply fine and dandy; but I didn't work in Georgia. I worked in Illinois at the Illinois branch of the facility. Did that mean that I would have to take a 1,600-mile trip from the Prairie State all the way to the Peach State to find a group of people in management who looked like me.

The "Hidden Bias," article goes on to say, "These shadows hang over stigmatized people no matter their status or accomplishments. They must remain on guard and bear an additional burden that may affect their self-confidence, performance, and aspirations. These stigmas have the potential to rob them of their individuality and debilitate their attempts to break out of stereotypical roles," (Teaching Tolerance, www.tolerance.org). Everyone can agree that one of the answers, once again is education, exposure and experience.

The Interview

During my first year at Purdue University, I applied for a Resident Assistant position, or RA position in the dorm. The Resident Assistant "facilitates the social, academic, and personal adjustment of students to the residence and University." When I attended Purdue, there were 33,000 Whites and 1,000 Blacks enrolled at the school.

The guy who interviewed me was the supervisor of RA's, but he was also a professor, in which school I can't remember. I do not know why I can't. It really was not that long ago. Laughing aloud!

I do however remember that he asked me what my mother did for a living at the start of the interview. I told him she was a teacher's aide at the elementary school that I had attended from first grade to eighth grade. He then asked me what my father did for a living, and I told him my father was a mail carrier and had worked for the post office for as long as I could remember. If only I had known at that time that my father graduated from high school at age fifteen, I would have thrown that in.

He also asked about my siblings' occupations. I only have one sister and she didn't get her first job until she was twenty-five years old, so I just said, "She doesn't work." The interviewer/professor proceeded to tell me—in no less than bragging terms—about his wife and children's prestigious jobs, including many of their other successes.

I'm sure I remember hearing the words doctor and lawyer at least once; or doctor twice, or something like that. For me it had become apparent incredibly early in the interview that the professor felt like I didn't measure up. You do not have to speculate as to whether I got the RA position. I did not. He ended the interview before ever asking me one question about my qualifications for the job.

Did I feel hurt and humiliated by the process? Of course, I did. Did I feel like he was stereotyping and showing bias toward my relatives who were hard working but not considered professionals? Would it have mattered if my parents were scientists or engineers, teachers or even doctors or lawyers? I do not think so.

In the article, "Hidden Bias," it states: *"A now classic experiment showed that White interviewers sat farther away from Black applicants than from White applicants and ended the interview 25% sooner. Such discrimination has been shown to diminish the performance of anyone treated that way, whether Black or White."* ("Hidden Bias: A Primer on Teaching Tolerance" www.tolerance.org)

Would I allow someone to treat me in the same way in an interview today? Absolutely not! But that does not mean that they will not try the same behavior. The difference today would be that I would be the one who would respectfully end the interview before it was done.

Children and Bias

"To work with another culture, we must first respect them, second, understand them and third, work within their frame of reference; their identities, values and myths."
(Awareness, CASA training presentation, Maryann Krieglstein, MSW, 1996)

I was visiting a neighbor one afternoon when a good friend of hers came for a visit. At the time, I was doing daycare in my home for school age children and happened to have my son and another preschooler with me. Both children were around four years old at the time.

When my neighbor's close friend entered the room, she exchanged a quick hello with the adults and then immediately zeroed in on my son. "He's so cute," she said, almost singing the words. The little preschooler standing with him was just as cute but she never complimented the little girl.

I tried to change the subject because the two children were standing right next to one another and she was unintentionally, I believe, ignoring the little girl and making a big fuss over my son. This was a time when I felt that a true assessment of her audience would have helped to temper her behavior.

After listening to her go on and on about how cute he was and feeling like I had said thank you at least 100 times, I became annoyed. My concern for the other child's feelings, coupled with the fact that she was oblivious to the fact that she was humiliating her, became almost more than I could take.

Before I knew it, I blurted out, "I get so tired of the Mississippi mentality that says if you're fairer skinned with semi straight hair, it makes you better looking." I had never been to Mississippi by that time so I didn't really know what the mentality there was, but I knew she was from the south and that I needed to say something that would get her attention immediately.

It wasn't just the whole, "to be light-skinned is better" mentality that was annoying me. It was also the fact that she didn't seem to have any regard for the way she was making the other little one feel. In addition, she seemed oblivious to the message she was sending to both children.

So now she's annoyed and she blurts out, "At least I didn't marry a white man!" I did not respond. At the time I didn't feel like I had the ammunition to argue her point and neither did I feel like I should be defending why I married my son's father while he was standing right there. If I had been given the chance to respond to her later, I would have said this:

I did not marry my husband because I thought he was better than anyone else. He was only better for me because after he swept me off my feet, I fell madly in love with him.

While I'm on the subject, I may as well venture into a few more things that are on my mind.

I do not believe Black men who marry White women are saying to Black women that they do not measure up or that they are not good enough. I do understand that there are exceptions to every rule, but I also believe that people should be able to marry the person they want to marry; no matter what color they are. If you have opened yourself up to get to know people in other cultures, you have a better opportunity to build relationships with people from other cultures.

I think that people who feel slighted when they see an interracial couple should reassess their own self-esteem, self-confidence, and self-worth. For me, the difference that stands out between me and any other race is culture and behavior. Culture gaps can be bridged, and behavior can change.

"I believe that by striving for a world that accepts it's oneness, we can transform wars, intolerance, religious persecution and political extremism into memory and maybe even folklore." (*Sargeant Ernesto Haibi, Medic with the 23rd Infantry Battalion in the National Guard*).

The other thing that is visibly and physically different is, of course, skin color and hair texture. That difference is a result of where we come from. Our skin color is related to the fact that some people came from hotter regions, and others came from climates where there was less sun. The people who have more melanin are also those who have thicker strands of hair but of course we already know this.

Not long after my little back and forth with my neighbor's friend, I began to tell the little girl that had experienced the affront, how beautiful she was. I continued to point out all of her best features until her face lit up light a Christmas tree.

Did my compadre believe that to be fairer-skinned is better? I can't be sure, but we need to be mindful of the message we are sending to our children. She might accuse me of sending the message that by marrying a White man, I think Black men do not measure up. On the contrary, I hope I am sending the message that adults should marry anyone they darn well please.

I mentioned earlier that my mother and father divorced when I very young. After that, my father did not continue as an active participant in my life. To give him some credit, he did show up every now and then but to give you an idea of what that was like, I can't say I ever had a "real" conversation with him. I mean I would talk, and he would not respond.

It was my single maternal uncle who filled in for my father when I was an adolescent. He eventually married and became unavailable as well. After he married, I adopted Martin Luther King Jr. as my newly appointed role model. It's a shame that I had so few positive male role models that I felt forced to latch on to someone I had never even met before.

Even worse, when Dr. King became my role model, he had already been assassinated, which makes me seem even more desperate by making the *memories* of an individual my role model. I latched on to everything I could about his memories and embraced them as if he were my own family member. Did I say he was my hero? He was my hero then, now and forever. I well up as I type the words.

I found Dr. King's intelligence to be so attractive. I always thought that he had to be the smartest man in the world. I mean, really, who graduates from high school at age fifteen. At my father's funeral, I learned that he had also graduated from high school at age fifteen. I think I learned everything I knew about my father at his funeral. These are the other things I learned about my father at his funeral:

As an undergraduate student, I was a communications major with emphasis on journalism. I was surprised to find out that my father had an Associate's degree in Journalism. My father was involved in airborne infantry when he was in the military. After the military he worked two jobs for more than thirty years.

I loved Martin Luther King Jr. I would have been willing to love my father as well if he had given me the opportunity; and just think of the things we could have chatted about if he had had the ability to open up.

I could have benefitted so much from a relationship with this person and with his attributes. If only he had made the effort, he would have become a very viable role model in my life as well.

Montessori

I used to work part-time at an all-white Montessori preschool. There were 102 children in the school and only one of the children was Black. When I was hired, I became the only Black staff at the school, and I was hired as a teacher's aide.

The little boy—who I will call Robert—was African American and was harassed mercilessly by the other kids daily. "What's wrong with your hair?" Why is your skin so dark?" The two teachers in the room did not take the opportunity to make this a teachable moment but sat silently by without saying a word.

They just behaved like this was normal, which I found out later that it was. It was a normal everyday occurrence.

One of the kids would start and it gave the other kids a license to chime in, "Why is your skin so dark?" Why does your hair feel like that?" Robert would respond calmly and say each time, "I don't know." Any variation of questions like these could be asked at various times as much as twenty or more times a day.

Since no other staff member seemed to ever rescue him, I often wondered if that was the reason for hiring me. I wonder if I was there to help Robert manage all the looks, the inappropriate touching, and the insults. There would be days when even I was overwhelmed by it. I was constantly forced to repeat the same thing over and over.

"Some people have darker skin and thicker hair," I would say. "Robert is still a very handsome boy."

"He's not handsome. He's ugly," would often be the response. "He's very handsome," I would repeat. "He is one of the most handsome boys I've ever seen." With that my little friend's eyes would light up and when staff was within earshot they would smile and light up as well.

Some days I would think to myself, "What kind of parent would put their child in a situation like this one when they are not equipped to defend themselves?" During the school's open house, I haphazardly expressed my concerns to Robert's mother. I must admit I wasn't clear in my communication.

I told her that the other children were very curious about Robert being different. I tried to explain (in a roundabout way) that at times this behavior made her son feel extremely uncomfortable. I do not know if she just didn't get it or she just didn't want to get it.

Robert continued to suffer through the anguish of having the kids question and humiliate him daily. There was no amount of explaining that seemed to divert their attention away from him being different. I could not take it. I left the school after being there for less than six months. I did talk to the administrator about the situation before I left, and she made me feel like she planned to fix it.

The moral of this story is not to send your young child to a school where they will be the "only" anything; not the only Black child; not the only LGBTQ child; not the only White child, the only Muslim child, etc. The only time I can see this working is if the staff plans to make the idea of differences teachable moments for all the students; even starting the lessons before the child comes for his or her first day.

Black Lives Matter Again

"We wouldn't have to have 'Black Lives Matter' if we hadn't had 300 years of Black lives don't matter," (Dorothy - Atalla@GoddessSpeaks).

"There's a group and movement that was formed [recently] called Black Lives Matter. It is an ideological and political intervention in a world where Black lives are systematically and intentionally targeted for demise. It is an affirmation of Black people's contributions to this society, our humanity, and our resilience in the face of deadly oppression." (*www.blacklivesmatterchicago.com*)

"The most poignant part of the Black odyssey was the ability of Africans to survive under the difficult circumstances of slavery and to manifest a lot of internal strength, and a lot of resolve," *African American culture* (*www.blackcollegiate.com*)

In "The Black Woman's Path to Mental Health," Marilyn Martin, M.D., M.P.H., says, "Black people are overrepresented in 'high-need' populations—people in prisons, psychiatric hospitals, inner cities and rural areas; and the people who are homeless."

Recently I had a remarkably interesting conversation with a girlfriend who happens to be White. We were out to lunch and although I'm rarely caught off guard, she managed to throw me a curve ball when she said, "What do you think of the organization, "Black Lives Matter."

I'm thinking… "Here we go." I was not sure I wanted to take the ride, but I knew trying to ward off the question was not an option either. I could have simply used a quote from Black Lives Matter. I could have said, "We do not want our children to be exempt from the law or above the law; what we are saying is we don't want them to be tried on the sidewalk."

But I didn't say that, and I felt unprepared for the question. I'm sure I pondered several minutes before saying, "I haven't given it much thought, but I guess now is as good a time as any to think about it." While I was still mulling over an appropriate answer, she hastened to let me know what she thought about the organization. I began to think she was more interested in telling me how she felt than about listening to my feelings.

She proceeded to tell me that Black people should be just as concerned about the loss of lives taken by stray bullets. In other words, she said she could not understand why Black people were so upset with the police when they were not protecting their loved ones from the violence perpetrated by Black-on-Black crime.

She said, "Aren't parents supposed to protect their kids from these types of occurrences as well?" She went on to say, "I'm not trying to give the police a pass for shooting innocent unarmed individuals, but I just feel that Black people should take responsibility for protecting their [own] homes and neighborhoods."

Wow! Let me just say first that I appreciate my friend's courage. I appreciate the fact that she feels comfortable enough with me to engage in dialogue about race. Most of my white friends are not that brave. Most people, no matter what color, are ever that brave.

Nevertheless, I did tell her that for those of us who have the proper parenting skills, we absolutely give 110% when it comes to keeping our children protected from harm. Yes, we could move into neighborhoods where stray bullets do not find their way into our homes, but unfortunately not all of us can afford that luxury.

Even with the best-laid plans and even for citizens who are not Black, things can go wrong. People lose the children they love through shootings, accidental drownings, car accidents, the accidental discharge of a firearm, etc. But to lose your unarmed love one to shots fired by a police officer is a totally separate set of circumstances, which I hope to address later in the book.

My girlfriend pressed on. She asked the question again, "Just tell me why people get upset about the police killing their loved ones and they don't protect their loved ones themselves." My disbelief for this kind of rationale was nothing short of shocking.

However, we were involved in dialogue, dialogue about race. Shocking or not, I do believe communication has the power to stop wars, so I pressed on as well. I wish I didn't have to tell you that my side of the communication increased significantly in intensity.

This is how I finally answered her question: "Maybe it's because for more than 100 or so years, the police, along with the Ku Klux Klan, have had a history of shooting, hanging, drowning, tarring and feathering, mutilating and burning to a stake any Black person who offended them or stood up for themselves.

My friend and I survived our exchange that day even though I admit to overreacting. But I come to the table with the remnants of slavery casting a shadow over my life. Like I stated earlier, my maternal grandmother was born in Alabama in 1906. I imagine that at some point there was a White man or woman who might have reprimanded her for even looking them in the eye.

I grew up in the house with that same grandmother who said things like, "Don't you dare look at me that way when I'm talking to you." I wanted to shout out, "How am I looking at you? And because I didn't know how I was looking at her, it was safer for me not to look at her at all when she was talking to me. In fact, I stopped looking at everyone when they talked to me. These are the remnants of racism. It would take another book to point it all out.

I have never witnessed a lynching, but I cannot stand to see anything hanging from a tree. At Halloween, if I see a witch, mummy, etc., hanging from a tree, it takes me back; it's as if I am connected to the souls of my ancestors and can feel a smidgen of the pain and agony they experienced.

The residual effects of slavery and racism still live on in our hearts and in our connection to those who lived and died before us: Those who died at the hands of people who were full of hate.

And then we are reminded that racism is not only residual but also alive and well when it's alleged that the alt-right supported Donald Trump in his race for the White House in 2016. "The Alternative Right, commonly known as the 'alt-right' is a set of far-right ideologies, groups and individuals whose core belief is that 'white identity' is under attack by multicultural forces using political correctness and social justice to undermine white people and their civilization." *(Southern Poverty Law Center; www.spleenter.org)*

I am further reminded of the hurt and hatred, when for the purposes of this book, I visited a white supremacy website and experienced the spewing of hatred in ways that I could not have imagined. I will share more about that experience later.

Black Men Matter Too

The Civil Rights movement was one of the toughest times that African Americans had to endure in my lifetime. We fell repeatedly, but we got back up again. We recovered, but some of us recovered scarred. This is my opinion, but the Black man is the last to recover from the scars of racism. This is not to say that there are not African American men who have not succeeded. I encounter those men every day.

As a culture, we believe what the Bible says about the man being the leader in the household. However, there are many circumstances that date back to slavery that have made it difficult for some Black men to take a leadership role in their households. That oppression, that still reigns after four hundred years, is destructive.

Our jails and penitentiaries are filled with Black and Brown men. Is it because they have all committed horrendous crimes or are the jails full because of what Joy DeGruy calls "Post Traumatic 'Slave' Syndrome in her book and book title?

I do not mean to say that offenders are not supported by public defenders. Some public defenders work hard on behalf of people who are unable to afford private attorneys, but it is not enough.

I have been there at the Will County courtroom observing as an intern when the white judge and the white attorney make a difference between the offenders who are shackled and handcuffed in the courtroom and those who come in with their private attorneys.

At times, it reminded me of the courtroom in To Kill a Mockingbird, originally a novel that made it to television about "growing up under extraordinary circumstances in the 1930's in the south."

I've seen the young white offender walk into the courtroom with his parents and I have seen the judge give the unshackled offender, who is also in a suit the proverbial "slap on the hand," with this as a warning, "Don't let me see you in my courtroom again."

Perhaps this wasn't your perspective the last time you were in court, but it was my personal observation. The shackled offenders who sit in the jury seats need only look around to see that the "playing field" is not level. Their visible circumstances make it clear that their chances of hearing the words, "I don't want to see you come into my courtroom again," are slim to none.

Did I mention that many of the men sitting in the jury box were always African American or Hispanic? The judge was White 99% of the time and every now and then a Black attorney would walk into the courtroom. Will County has handled more than 20,000 adult felony cases, 18,000 misdemeanor/traffic cases and more than 1000 juvenile cases in 2014. At the time of this writing, the Public Defender's office had three African American public defenders, two male and one female. *(willcountypublicdefender.com)*

While attending a Cook County Jail Ministry spring dinner at Oak Park Baptist Church, a representative from Cook County jail spoke to the audience. He informed us that Cook County Jail would be adding a new wing, which is preparation for individuals who, today, are in the first grade.

In other words, jail administrators know that in 10 to 15 years (considering the institution's past growth), the jail needs to prepare for that larger number of individuals who will be available to house as offenders in the future.

It does not matter if you are young or old, if you are a Black man, you're catching pure H-E-double hockey sticks on the racism circuit. I have worked or been employed with many Black men who were blatantly disrespected by a White supervisor on a job site. In each case, the guy being reprimanded did not utter a mumbling word in response.

On a couple of occasions, when I witnessed the disrespect for myself, I was tempted to stand up on behalf of my coworkers and I would have eventually if I had stayed on either job long enough. On one of the jobs I am referring to, I had a White supervisor tell me that a monkey could do my job. I chose not to respond but as the millennials would say, "It was time to bounce."

After each incident with my coworkers, I was curious about why they chose not to stand up for themselves. I got an opportunity to ask each one of them. In both cases the answer was somewhere along the line of, "It's not worth the trouble." One guy was sure that he would be fired if he said anything. This was the same job where the same supervisor told me at a staff meeting that a monkey could do my job.

But this was not even the last straw for me. The last straw for me was when the same Black male coworker and a White female coworker had a disagreement and got involved in a back-and-forth exchange of harsh words.

This woman had harsh verbal exchanges with everyone. It was extremely hard to have a good relationship with her. I was startled when, in the middle of the exchange, the supervisor started yelling at the male coworker. "Shut up! Shut your mouth! I don't want to hear anymore!" I was mortified.

Silence fell over the room. I thought to myself, "does this guy understand the implications of his behavior." He was yelling at a college educated African American adult in front of his peers. First, he was treating him as if he were talking to a child and second, he was talking to him as if we were living during 1909 instead of 2009. I wanted nothing more than to give the supervisor a piece of my mind.

I knew that I didn't want the job anymore. I believe that during the time he was putting this coworker in his place, he was trying to send a message to me as well. They had already told me that a monkey could do my job and even that didn't make me feel as bad as I did for my coworker that day. The incident broke my heart.

On one of my first jobs ever, I worked for a family-owned paint company. They hired men who were justice involved to clean paint off different articles and it was a dirty job. It was the kind of job that no one would want to do. It was a last resort job for people that were under last resort circumstances.

When the guys were not working, they were not allowed to interact or even look at the other employees. I hated the way they were being treated. It was as if they were still in prison or worse. I felt like they had been completely stripped of any shred of dignity.

These guys were not allowed in the building and had to deal with extremely hot and wintry weather conditions outside. One day, when I had to take something out to them to be cleaned, I exchanged one or two sentences with them which was a "How are you," and a "Thanks and have a good day."

The owner's daughter must have been looking out the window. She came outside and started yelling and telling the men they had no business talking to me. I do not think they did talk to me. I talked, and they only smiled. "You know better," she said. "If it happens again, you'll be out of here."

I felt myself losing it. I could not believe how she was treating the men. She was degrading them so terribly in my presence; talking to them like most people wouldn't talk to their pets. Before I knew it, I yelled, "Who do you think you are?" Do you think these guys don't deserve to be treated like human beings?"

And now I am screaming at the top of my lungs. "You're a monster! Just because these guys have spent time in prison you think that gives you a license to treat them like dogs?"

I didn't look in the direction of the guys, but I imagine they were silently rejoicing because someone had said the things they had been thinking. When she recovered from the initial shock of my words, she burst into tears. I took off my gear, threw it on a table and exited the building. I was glad that I was able to just walk away, but I was sorry for the people who couldn't.

When I worked at a residential school in Glen Ellyn, I hired more African American males than they ever had work at the school. Our deaf/blind students were bussed to other suburban schools in the area for their day program and for activities that provided inclusion. All the schools we were assigned to were predominantly White and that included the student and staff population.

Occasionally we would get calls at our home school from our area schools saying one of our aides, one of our Black male staff, had forgotten their ID and were not being allowed to enter the school.

Let me see, you go to the same school five days a week. You drive up to that school in the same school bus with the same disabled children to arrive at the place where you work every day. Strangely enough, if I forgot my ID, they never even noticed.

Unfortunately, racism rears its ugly head in several distinct aspects and forms. Most people who have been discriminated against feel that they have experienced some of the worst forms of racism, but in my lifetime, I believe Black men have had the toughest times in our society to date.

Shali Tilson, a 22-year-old African American man "being detained while Black" died in the Rockdale County Jail in March 2018 after being arrested for a misdemeanor charge. Tilson died in custody nine days after his arrest. An autopsy indicated complications from dehydration caused Tilson's death. The camera showed Tilson push the call button in his cell several times, bang on the cell door, and try to climb the wall the day he died.

Trayvon Martin, a 17-year-old African American youth from Miami Gardens, Florida, was "walking while Black" on February 26, 2012 when he was fatally shot by George Zimmerman after Zimmerman called 911 to report a "suspicious person" in the neighborhood. Zimmerman was initially charged with murder but was later acquitted of all charges.

Aumaud Arbery, a 25-year-old African American, was "jogging while Black" on February 23, 2020 in Brunswick,

Georgia when he was cornered and fatally shot by two local townsmen, Travis McMichael and Gregory McMichael. The two McMichael's, who are father and son, are facing murder and aggravated assault charges. "William Bryan, who filmed the video, is facing charges of criminal attempt to commit false imprisonment."

Bridging the Gap

When I joined Facebook a few years ago I also became a tweeter by joining the social media network Twitter. The tweeting and Facebook experience has allowed me to connect with people from all around the world. I have met people with cultural differences, religious differences and people with opinions that differ from my own.

So far, through my tweeting experiences, I've connected with a person who is an ex-mob boss who spent years in prison but has since turned his life around and is now making a positive difference in the world.

I, for one, cannot wait to see that change in the world that Dr. Martin Luther King Jr. spoke of in his "I Have a Dream" speech when he said, "...all of God's children, Black men and White men, Jews and gentiles Protestants and Catholics, will all join hands..."

I have that same dream that as a nation, one day we will become more tolerant of one another, that we will open our hearts and minds to people who are different. That we will really begin to understand what it means to "love thy neighbor."

I dream that one day we will finally realize that we don't have all the answers and that another person's opinion, religion, and social status can be celebrated simply because they are different.

There are tweeters from all walks of life on the web who have been very open and gracious. They say things like, "Look me up on Facebook," or "Come and check out my blog," or "I love meeting new people, send me a message anytime."

Through my interaction with these individuals, I can see barriers breaking down, people becoming more tolerant and individuals coming together in ways that never would have been possible. Twitter is even bridging the gap between the celebrity and the working-class man or woman.

I have been blessed to have a lot of friends, most of whom are compatible with me because of our similarities. But one friend, Gary Handwerg, is extra special because we have almost nothing in common. Our bond is a true lesson in tolerance. Our most obvious difference is he's White and I'm Black. Nowadays, this is not so unusual but what's more unusual for us is where we "look like" we came from.

When we are together in the car or on the street, people always do double takes. Drivers have looked around their passengers to get a look into my car when my friend and I are riding together. My friend admits to having an eccentric look. He hasn't cut his beard in more than twenty years and it hangs halfway down his chest. If he put on a Santa Claus suit, he could pull off Santa in a heartbeat.

One of our mutual friends describes us as the city slicker and the guy from the hills. She insists (in a halfway joking way) that when people see us together, they think he's the rich eccentric and I must be trying to swindle him out of his money.

Quite the contrary is true. As different as we are from one another, we have found commonalities in our relationship. I remember one day bantering back and forth with him in a grocery store about who grew up the poorest.

I had pointed out a package of neck bones in the meat section of the store and said to my friend, "We ate a lot of those when I was a kid because they were cheap, and we were poor." He said, "If you were able to buy meat, you weren't that poor. He said, "I guess we were poorer that poor," and the two of us got a good laugh. We enjoy each other's company because I tolerate his uniqueness as we celebrate our differences.

This friend is super smart. In fact, his IQ or intelligence quotient is close to genius. The last time I looked, I found myself to be somewhere around hmm...average intelligence. But this difference does not deter him from making me look good in the intelligence department. He will spend hours explaining a subject (until I'm exhausted). He accepts who I am, and I accept who he is.

I love spending time with people and my friend prefers computers or even animals to people. Social events tend to confuse him because he has not attended enough for his age. He spent a lot of years living with and taking care of his mom, watching sixty hours of television a week and ignoring the outside world.

I love dining out and he has only tasted one or two salad dressings in his life. I can eat salad three times a day and he thinks salad and its ingredients are for rabbits. Before I became a vegetarian, chicken wings were one of my favorite foods. My friend describes chicken wings as bones with a little meat and he refuses to eat them.

His favorite food is boiled hamburger and macaroni without anything added besides salt. I love to cook, and he prefers most of his meals straight from a can. He is guided by the universe and I am guided by God. I remain open minded with him and he remains open minded with me. I love music and he interprets music as noise. I am respectful of his feelings and he is respectful of mine.

Although we have few things in common, I would give him the shirt off my back, and he would give me the shirt off his. Even though the nature of our friendship is decorated with differences, through our union as friends, I believe he has taught me to be even more tolerant, patient and accepting. As a result, I hope I am even more respectful and loving as I celebrate the differences in others who live in our world.

I recently lost my buddy, my brother, my friend Gary to one of the deadliest types of brain cancers called Glioblastoma multiforme (GBM). His sudden and unexpected illness and subsequent death was devastating. Memories of our times together will be forever in my heart.

∞

Intolerance is alive and well in this country and abroad. It is as prevalent today as it was 100 years ago. We are still confused about what it means to "love thy neighbor." Several of us still believe that loving our neighbor means loving those who look like us, are in the same socioeconomic place that we are in or can meet us on the golf course at our favorite country club.

And of course, if all lives matter, then loving our neighbor means loving people in those groups as well.

However, it also means loving your African American neighbor, your homeless neighbor, your Atheist neighbor, your Christian neighbor, your disabled neighbor, your LGBTQ neighbor, your neighbor who suffers from addiction, your neighbor who has been justice involved, your neighbor who holds a different world view and even your neighbor who may be a white nationalist.

"When you teach a man to hate and fear his brother [or neighbor], when you teach that he is a lesser man because of his color or his beliefs or the policies he pursues, when you teach that those who differ from you threaten your freedom, or your job or your family, then you also learn to confront others not as fellow citizens but as enemies. We must recognize that this short life can neither be enabled (nor) enriched by hatred or revenge." Robert F. Kennedy (adapted)

Intolerance hurts. And you didn't miss it when I alluded to the fact that the behavior of some is as bad today as it was one hundred years ago. I wasn't here 100 years ago, but I still have enough wisdom to know that we have not made a lot of progress in the "tolerance" department. Also, because I am your African American neighbor, and have been around the block on this journey called life, I know how it feels to be discriminated against and purposely hurt just because of the color of my skin.

I have looked back at some of the trailblazers I admire that were successful despite the abusive racial tension that they had to endure. People like self-made millionaire Madam C.J. Walker, Booker T. Washington, Harriet

Tubman, Dr. Martin Luther King Jr., Rosa Parks and Barack Obama, to name a few.

When I think of the trails they have had to blaze, I am so grateful for the doors that opened because of their diligence and tenacity. I am grateful to every African American before me who fought tirelessly to secure voters' rights, the right to own property and even the right to sit anywhere we want on a city bus; with one of our longest won fights being to secure the 44th presidency of the United States of America.

I'm so grateful to the people who fought to have doors opened for me, for my children and for my great grandchildren. Let us not forget that as I put pen to page, there are white supremacy websites that are spewing hate. And these people do not just spend their lives in their homes, they are out in your community and mine.

I saw this post on Facebook: The caption read, "Why Does the Klan Wear Hoods:" The posted answer was: "Because when they're done, they go back to be your doctors, your lawyers, your governors, your police officers, your senators, your congressmen and women, your teachers, your judges, your co-workers, etc."

I was in a dentist office as a new patient and the dental hygienist was trying to talk me into an electric toothbrush kit that at the time had a $200 price tag. I respectfully declined. When the dentist entered the room and found that I would not buy the product, he said, "If you don't care about your dental care, why should I? He then started yelling, "Get out! Get out!"

I was so confused that it took me a minute to really figure out what was going on. I got up and went to the front desk to see if I could get a reasonable explanation from the receptionist. Before I could say anything to her, the dentist came out into the reception area and started yelling, "Get out now before I call the police." It was one of the most bizarre experiences I have ever encountered. All I can say is…the posted answer as to why the "Klan wears hoods" should have also included 'dentists' as well.

By now, someone is thinking, "Black people can be racist too. Sure, we can but let me make this clear: The White person is our neighbor; my neighbor and yours; therefore, intolerance toward them is unacceptable; completely unacceptable as well. As I always say, and this is *my* quote: *When we are prejudice against those who are prejudice against us, we miss the whole point."*

My next-door neighbor is white. As I said earlier, she doesn't give me the time of day. But you better believe if she ever needs me for anything, her behavior towards me would not have a bearing on my response to her. I am ready with an overflowing cup of love for her if she would ever give me the opportunity.

Someone posted a scripture on Facebook once that read: *"And this commandment we have from him: Whoever loves God must also love his brother."* I reposted and added these words; words that came sincerely: "It is not optional."

I acknowledge that Black people can be intolerant and can be guilty of not loving their neighbors. Sometimes, however, it's a result of our pain over that intolerance that is always pointed in our direction. I have personally spoken to some truly angry African Americans; some of us came out of the trenches wounded more deeply than others. Nevertheless, all of us have a responsibility to show love.

There was a librarian at the public school that I attended when I was in second grade. She was white, but I didn't know that at the time. It was not because I had a visual impairment of any kind but according to my maternal grandmother, I was continually reminded that I should never trust a white person. This librarian didn't look like anyone who couldn't be trusted so in my adolescent mind, it never occurred to me that she was white.

This elementary school librarian I'm referring to was so kind that there was just no way she could be one of the people my grandmother talked about. My mother worked at the same school as a teacher's aide, and I remember hearing her tell someone that Ms. Hillbruner was one of only three White staff at the school.

Later, I asked my Mom if Ms. Hillbruner was white. She assured me that she *was* White and seemed to be a bit perplexed by my confusion. "She doesn't look White to you?" she asked. How could I say that she looked White but couldn't be White because of my grandmother's description of White people?

During my eight years in elementary school, Ms. Hillbruner had an incredibly positive impact on my life. She may even be part of the reason that one of my favorite places to be is in the library. I loved Mrs. Hillbruner as much as I loved Father Joy.

Father Joy and the Catholic Church were responsible for a lot of positive aspects that shaped my life. One of those things included being involved in Girl Scouting, and the other was my participation in Harambee, The School of Human Dignity.

Becoming a Girl Scout was one of the most important highlights of my young life. I can still recite the preamble and take extraordinary pride in doing so: "On my honor I will try to do my duty to God and my country, to help other people at all times, and to obey the Girl Scout law." I credit all my good feelings about scouting to great leaders and to an awesome scouting education.

One of my scouting experiences went very wrong and I have never uttered a word about it to anyone until now. I believe it would have killed my mother if I told her what happened to me at my only weekend overnight scouting experience.

When I arrived at the campground, which was more than an hour from my home, I was extremely excited and not at all apprehensive about being left as my mother returned to her vehicle, drove off and returned home.

I was eight years old and the only Black child in my group of about six or seven other girls. There were three camp counselors who were all White as well. As I type these words, I am surprised at the emotion that is welling up in me because of the pain this caused so long ago.

I joined my group, and we were given some time to get to know one another. My feelings of discomfort in the group were immediate. As a child, I had been the only Black person in situations before, but I had never felt so out of place. With my other experiences, color did not create a barrier to love.

The White people I had encountered up to that point knew how to love their neighbor. They knew how to pour love into the hearts of others. But this Girl Scout group only had knowledge of how to empty the love tanks of others.

There was a little girl in our group who already was a leader or take-charge person at an early age. She seemed to be the most popular as well, and she was totally in control of me as well as all the other girls.

She told me that I would be her slave and she also explained what that would mean. I felt privileged to be getting attention because I believe the decision to ignore me had already been established by all the others. On our first hike, she instructed me to walk behind her. She told me I would carry her things, throw away her trash, wipe the dirt off her shoes and eat my food in silence.

My naiveté about being in an uncomfortable social setting and my desire to be included helped to lead me down this very dark road. But I was smart enough to know, especially since the other girls had decided to ignore me, that this would be the only way to get any attention from my scouting peers during my time spent at the campsite.

On the second day of my weekend scouting experience, I remember sharing our lunch table with a host of houseflies. They were everywhere. The tuna sandwiches the camp counselor put in front of me was attracting the flies like bees to honey. One fly after another landed on my sandwich.

When it was time to go, I told the camp counselor I did not want the sandwich. She told me if I didn't eat it, I would not get anything else to eat. I felt like that was okay until she also forbade me to have my chips, fruit and my drink.

I was confused, hurt and hungry. The counselors talked among themselves about how I was overreacting and "that the flies hadn't hurt the sandwich." I heard one counselor say, "She has some nerve." It is true that the other girls ate their sandwiches. I was not trying to act like I was better than anybody else, but I knew flies also spent time on dog poop and I just didn't want any part of that.

That evening the scouts were given campground chores. I was told I would be cleaning the outhouse on Saturday and Sunday morning while the other girls had chores like picking up wood, making sure the cabin was clean, etc. They also had each other around while they cleaned. I went to the outhouse alone. My eyes are moistening as I write this and even again when I reread it.

I took my bucket of water and my towels and I cleaned the toilet and the handles and the door. I even wiped down the walls. Again, flies were everywhere; the smell was horrible. What was even worse was being alone and a river of sadness washed over me. Nevertheless, I wanted to do my best.

One of the counselors checked my work and complimented me. I was happy to have any positive feedback at that campground. Today I believe they must have laughed when they thought of how difficult it must have been for me to be closed in the outhouse with the horrific smells and the flies.

I never said a word about my negative campground experience to my mother. When I returned home, I heard my mother as she bragged on one telephone conversation about me having the opportunity to go away to Girl Scout camp. I didn't say anything because I wanted her to feel good about making the financial sacrifice on my behalf. I know if I had shared any one of my horrible experiences it would have been equivalent to driving a knife into her heart.

Even if I had waited and shared the information years later, she would have still been devastated. No mother can stand to see her children hurt by anyone, anywhere, at any time, especially when the motivation is intolerance because someone is different.

For me, the moral of this story is to be careful where you send your children. It may be comfortable for you to put them in a situation where no one looks like them but how comfortable will it be for your child? It is important that we stay cognizant of that...even today.

In addition to scouting, Father Joy was responsible for my attending Harambee, The School of Human Dignity. During the time that I was involved with Harambee, we engaged in many activities; one of which was going on field trips. On one of those field trips, we attended a function at the Rainbow PUSH Coalition, led by the Reverend Jesse Jackson, Sr.

I remember gathering on the streets in an area that could have been downtown Chicago or an area just south of the

Loop where we stood on the street with a lot of other people shouting, "Say it loud, I'm Black and I'm proud."

At the same time, we held our fists high in the air, which symbolized the black power salute. This symbol was widely used by the Black Panther party in the 1960's as an expression of solidarity, strength or defiance. Although I felt like I wanted nothing more than to be Black and proud, I felt embarrassed by the whole thing. I didn't know at the time that the experience would impact my life in a positive and meaningful way.

It was meant to build my self-confidence and self-esteem and teach me not to compromise my dignity. It did all that and more.

As a kid, I did not know that people's behavior towards me could just be the result of our differences. I didn't understand until long after some of my experiences that Father Joy enrolled me in The School of Human Dignity because he had my self-esteem, self-worth, and best interest at heart. Maybe if I had attended Harambee before the scouting experience, things would have turned out different. Unfortunately, I will never know.

The Life of the Homeless Person Matters

I am not presently homeless, but I have shared some beautiful moments with people who are. Individuals in the homeless community have also motivated me. For most of my adult life, I have volunteered at homeless shelters with my church, on my own and with one of the ministry groups when I attended Lewis University in Romeoville, Illinois.

My experience during my tour of duty as a homeless shelter volunteer included work in three Illinois communities: Joliet, Chicago and at a PADS, Public Action to Deliver Shelter, facility in Wheaton. These shelters were in Will, Cook and DuPage County because I am an equal opportunity volunteer.

I would be remiss if, while talking about homelessness and the homeless community, I did not mention or counter what I hear on a regular basis from people who do not understand the culture of homelessness at all. There is this general belief that homeless people want to be homeless. I hear it time and time again. "People are homeless because they want to be."

As ludicrous as it sounds, some people who are not homeless believe that there are homeless people in this world who have chosen homelessness over being comfortable and warm and secure in a home or apartment of their own.

Nothing is further from the truth. Homelessness is one of the most difficult predicaments a person can encounter. In a bout with homelessness myself, I was able to stay with one friend after another until I got back on my feet. In other words, I have enough friends to be able to couch surf, but everyone is not that fortunate.

Even under these circumstances and with a vehicle, my belongings ended up lost and all over the place; but mostly in places where I was unable to find them when I needed them. When I needed to apply for a job, I had to find a place for all my things outside of my Ford Escort hatchback.

At that time, there was nothing worse, to me, than being homeless and advertising it when you drive into the parking lot of the place where you're being interviewed, with a car that is chugged full of your belongings.

The other misconception about homelessness is that people must want to be on the street because there are shelters they could go to have a warm place and a cot to sleep on. Some people feel their only option is the street. Why? Because they have been kicked out of the shelter for one reason or another, they find the shelter to be too restrictive because of so many rules or they are distrustful of the other people at the shelter.

As a rule, when I do not have to worry about a place to stay, I feel capable and positive. My self-diagnosed attention deficit disorder or ADD can at times allow me to accomplish as much in a day as two people. Not because I am more capable but because sometimes I'm just "all over the place," and I have learned how to use it to my advantage.

On the other hand, there are times when I get tired and discouraged. That is when my homeless friends become my role models, my motivation, my encouragement, and my heroes.

Most people might agree that people who are homeless do not see themselves in the position of role models or world heroes. People who are not homeless are unaware that in the culture of homelessness there are many success stories.

The strength and tenacity that some individuals in the homeless community exhibit is impressive. There are some homeless people who would run circles around those of us who have never had to work as hard to just survive.

On some of my worst days, I have been jerked up by my bootstraps when a friend who is homeless announces, "I'm taking college courses." On another day, I might hear, "I got an apartment" or "I got a job yesterday."

"My daughter is finally in daycare."

"I just got my new car."

"I've been drug free for six months."

I have a homeless friend who has four children. She is the rock of Gibraltar. She was forced to leave her home because of physical and emotional abuse that she endured while living with her husband. I applaud her determination, but her daily challenges are many. I will call her Sarah.

Sarah had been homeless a few months when I first met her. She attended work while three of her older children attended school. Her youngest child was temporarily being cared for by another person at the PADS day shelter and the caregiver of the little one was also homeless.

A typical week in Sarah's life included time at her job and time at the PADS day site until it closed at 6:00 p.m. After 6:00 p.m. Sarah traveled with her children to night shelters at surrounding local area churches.

Each night the location was different because certain churches took responsibility for housing the homeless overnight on certain nights of the week. In a week, Sarah traveled with her children to five churches that were spread over five suburban towns in DuPage County.

On weekends, the day site is closed, so Sarah would sit with her four children at a local train station. She sometimes spent the entire day at the train station waiting for the night shelters to open at 7:00 p.m. On Monday morning Sarah traveled back to the day site on foot with her four young children in tow.

When Sarah would arrive at the site on Monday, she would start her day by getting her three older children ready for school. This could sometimes mean working around as many as twenty-five or more homeless individuals at the day shelter.

Despite the obstacles, Sarah persevered and continued to achieve a goal of making steady progress in her life. She is one of my role models, a source of inspiration and my hero.

One weekend, when Sarah was able to afford a hotel room, she invited me over for a visit. We had a grand time together. We laughed. We cried. We shared beautiful moments. I have had many of these moments throughout the years. I will never forget some of them.

I recently attended a training session for another volunteer program. During the session, I learned about different behaviors in various cultures. As I sat listening to the speaker, I couldn't help but think that the homeless community deserved to be recognized as a culture of its own.

It is a community with unique cultural experiences. It is diverse and distinctive. It is where difficult moments are overcome. But it is also where beautiful moments can be made. It is a place where the homeless individual can become the hero.

On the other hand, the homeless community can also be a place where only the strong survive. It can be a place where people feel like they're hanging by a thread and must make a daily decision to either keep hanging on or to just let go.

In my work with men who are justice involved, I am up close and personal with homelessness every day. When I hear stories of people having to ride the train all night, stories of being beat up and robbed, stories of having to lay in front of a city bus during rush hour to get people's attention because you're hungry, I am humbled.

It is my responsibility to tell you, my reader, that homelessness has a lot more downs than ups. This is my made-up statistic, but I would venture to guess that half of the men I worked with coming out of Cook County Jail, had been homeless at one time or another.

Because my job at the Supportive Release Center entailed spending entire overnights with guys released from Cook County Jail, I had the privilege of hearing stories about many of their experiences related to time living on the street. Sometimes a few of the men would say they were relieved when they were arrested. If they had been riding the train all night or sleeping in parks, "the jail" would give them a comfortable and safe place to sleep.

There were complaints about noise at the jail but a few of the guys said they were comfortable knowing they would be safer with the correctional officers than they were at night alone on the street. It is always hard to hear that being in jail is a better option than being out of jail but I completely understand.

I met a person who had been arrested on several occasions and said that eighteen of his arrests were for trespassing. It is difficult for adult men who are homeless to find a safe dry place to be when they don't have money.

One of my clients, that I mentioned earlier, said he was so hungry and frustrated that once he laid down in front of a (CTA) Chicago Transit Authority bus during morning rush hour. He said some of the passengers got off the bus with the driver to find out what was going on.

He said he told them he was diabetic and needed to eat. In his words, "everyone was passing him money." He also said he was not sure if they were motivated more by his situation or by the fact that they wanted to get to work.

Another homeless client was arrested for going into cars to find change to buy something to eat. He was not a drug user; his behavior was motivated by hunger. He told me he had been a ward of the state his entire life and admitted to not having any real attachments to any one of his foster parents.

He was twenty-one years old, intelligent as well as forth coming. He was tall and clean cut. During the time we spent together he admitted talking to me more than he had ever talked to anyone.

He told me that he did not have any felony convictions, so I begged him to find legal alternatives to securing cash when he needed something, especially food. I tried to assure him that people are more sensitive when they think you're hungry as opposed wanting money for drugs and alcohol.

I assured him that because of his intellect and his ability to keep himself looking nice and clean cut, people would help if he would just say he was hungry. I pleaded with him to promise me he would ask for help instead of breaking the law.

In the end, we couldn't place this young person in any long-term housing situation because he did not abuse drugs or alcohol. We did end up taking him to a homeless shelter where, my guess is, he didn't stay very long.

The Life of the Homeless Teen Matters

Accordingccording to the National Center on Family Homelessness, there are 1.6 million homeless youth in the United States. Many associated risk factors have been identified for adolescent homelessness, including family conflict, leaving foster care, running away, being thrown away, physical or sexual abuse and coming out to parents as lesbian, gay, bisexual or transgender. (*Lost in the Shuffle: Culture of Homeless Adolescents, Oliveira, Burke, 2009*).

Child abuse accounts for 2000 fatalities a year in the United States. (*Child Welfare Information Gateway, 2009*). According to the U.S. Department of health and Human Services, "One or both parents are responsible for 69.9 percent of this abuse, and more than one quarter (27.1%) of these fatalities are perpetuated by the mother alone."

Most child abuse statistics focus on the younger child. As a result, the older child or teenager is not only left to fend for him or herself, but also left with limited solutions for solving the problem of escaping abuse in the home. For some, foster care can become an option; for others, living with neighbors or friends can become an option.

Other homeless adolescents continue to devise their own method for combating or preventing further abuse and neglect. Their simple answer, which can become extremely complicated for the adolescent, is to run away. This has become the solution for thousands of teens that run away every day.

"Children who flee to the streets are often ones who are not going to take it anymore, whether the 'it' is sexual or physical abuse or severe psychological and emotional neglect and abuse." (*Article: Early child maltreatment, runaway youths, and risk of delinquency and victimization in adolescence: A mediational model, MJ Kim, EA Tajima, EI Herrenkohl, B Huang, 2009*).

Teen homelessness and victimization is an equal opportunity phenomenon that spreads across all racial and ethnic backgrounds. Street victimization is defined as being robbed, beat up, sexually assaulted, or sexually abused (when a youth is under the age of 18) by an adult. The victimization of teens in the home can lead to further abuse on the street. (*Journal of the American Academy of Child and Adolescent Psychiatry: Victimization and Posttraumatic Stress Disorder Among Adolescents: Whitbeck, Chen, Hoyt, Tyler, Johnson, 2004*).

According to the Department of Justice, every year 1.7 million teens experience homelessness in the United States. Adolescents who are left to fend for themselves on the street and have nowhere to turn can be exposed to several high-risk situations. They can also find themselves using inappropriate mechanisms to survive.

Stressors for homeless youth entail drug use and abuse, engaging in survival sex, dealing with mental health issues that lead to depression, post-traumatic stress disorder and in extreme cases, suicide.

The Voices of Youth Count from Chapin Hall at the University of Chicago also found that:

- One in ten young adults ages 18-25 and at least 30 adolescents, ages 13-17 experience some form or homelessness unaccompanied by a parent or guardian over the course of a year.
- Twenty-nine percent of homeless youth report having substance misuse problems.
- Sixty-nine percent of homeless youth report mental health problems.
- Thirty-three percent had once been part of the foster care system.
- Fifty percent of homeless youth have been in the juvenile justice system, in jail or detention.
- Sixty-two percent of lesbian, gay, bisexual, transgender, queer, and questioning LGBTQ youth report being physically harmed while experiencing homelessness while 47% of non-LGBTQ youth reported being physically harmed while homeless.
- The lack of high school diploma or General Equivalency Diploma (GED) is a number one correlate for elevated risk or youth homelessness.
  (Voices of Youth Count, Chapin Hall, University of Chicago).

Sociology professors Kimberly Tyler and Morgan Beal, point out in the article, The High-Risk Environment of Homeless Young Adults, that navigating the streets for young runaways can prove to be extremely problematic:

"Survival on the streets frequently means adapting deviant strategies to meet physical, emotional, economic and safety needs, as well as to sustain some sense of home and sanity. *(Article, The High-Risk Environment of Homeless Young Adults: Consequences of Physical and Sexual Victimization, Tyler, Beal, 2010).*

Surviving on the street for the homeless or runaway youth can mean having to engage in deviant behavior, as well as having to interact with deviant peers. Additionally, survival often means early sexual abuse under the auspices of engaging in survival sex to make money for necessities. Survival for the teen can also mean that to feel sane the youth will begin to self-medicate or abuse drugs and alcohol to forget the stresses that come with living on the street.

"Despite the method of medicating, there is still a high incidence of suicide among homeless youth. Living on the street can lead to depression, elevated levels of anxiety, post-traumatic stress syndrome and suicide." *(Whitbeck, Hoyt, Johnson, Chen, 2004).*

Homeless youth are said to use drugs to ease their mind from the struggles of life on the street. Most of the youth on the street who take drugs use the substances as a coping mechanism. Researchers point out, however, that drugs and alcohol can be responsible for an increase in deviant behavior. In addition, if an adolescent is struggling with depression and thoughts of suicide, using drugs, especially alcohol, will give the young person the courage they need to follow through with that behavior.

Survival Sex

Homeless adolescents use survival sex on the street for obvious reasons. According to research, girls are more likely to engage in survival sex than boys. LGBTQ adolescents, as stated earlier, are more likely to engage in survival sex than straight teens.

Straight females and gay males are more likely to engage in survival sex. Also, as the youth increases in age, the likelihood of engaging in survival sex increases 1.5 times. "If the youth has been abused by a caretaker and has spent time directly on the street, each increases the likelihood of using survival sex by two times. The most potent predictor, however, was meeting criteria for conduct disorder, which increased the likelihood of survival sex more than thirteen times. *(Whitbeck, Chen, Hoyt, Tyler, Johnson, 2004).*

According to an article in the American Public Health Association Journal entitled Prevalence and Correlates of Survival Sex Among Runaway and Homeless Youth, "An abusive family environment is a risk factor that can encourage participation in survival sex once a youth is on the street."

While volunteering at a juvenile detention center, I met several female detainees who were repeat runaways. In each case, through sit down talks and/or interviews with the youth, it was determined that some of the girls' repeated runs were a result of abuse they were experiencing in the home.

In a couple of cases these female teens had been removed from their homes (because of their running) and placed in foster care. When they returned to the place where they were being abused, they would run again. It became a vicious cycle for some of the teens.

It is interesting to note that these girls did not divulge information about the abuse to the staff social worker, mental health professionals or nurses at the facility, but instead opened up to me as a volunteer. However, in some cases, when the abuse was reported to staff, the teens said there had been no follow up because of the reports.

No follow up could mean further victimization for the teen when they returned home. One teen that divulged information about her abuse at home, returned to the detention center (for running away) on two more occasions. The upheaval caused by repeatedly transitioning from home to detention caused her to start acting out. She would go back and forth from explosive episodes to visible signs of depression.

Post-Traumatic Stress Disorder (PTSD) and Suicide

Living on the street can cause depression, post-traumatic stress disorder (PTSD) and suicide. PTSD as defined in the Diagnostic and Statistical Manual occurs when an individual has been in a traumatic event that is outside the range of human experience.

Things "outside the range of human experience" would be fighting in a war while serving in the military, being in a car accident, witnessing a murder or being involved in a rape. (*BehaveNet Clinical Capsule: Post Traumatic Stress Disorder Handout*).

I have volunteered at Chicago area homeless shelters my entire adult life. I have spent more than twenty years as well fostering children, which resulted in three adoptions. While volunteering at the DuPage County Juvenile Detention Center through a program called Jumpstart, I tutored and mentored teens who's well-being I am still concerned about today.

As a former foster parent, homeless shelter volunteer and juvenile detention volunteer, I have seen teenagers from many backgrounds and cultures who come out of abusive homes, with broken hearts and unpredictable futures. Today I see teens in similar situations coming out of Cook County Jail, Department of Corrections, whose futures have been dimmed by abuse and homelessness. It is times like these that make me feel overwhelmed and at times powerless.

The Foster Child Matters

According to ifoster.org "the state of foster care is constantly changing and evolving. No two years – or even months – are exactly the same but they do hold to a few foster care statistics:

- There are approximately 440,000 foster youth nationwide.
- Thirty thousand youth age out of the foster care system between the ages of 18—21 annually.
- Within four years of aging out, 50% have no earnings, and those who do make an average annual income of $7,500.
- Only 5% of rural foster youth and 21% of urban foster youth report access to a computer at home.
- The median age of children in foster care is 6 ½ years old.
- The price of underinvesting in our foster youth results in $1 million in societal costs.

These statistics were a large part of what motivated me to become an adoptive parent. I adopted because I wanted to do something about abortion. I adopted because I wanted to do something to combat child abuse. I adopted because I wanted to do something about homelessness. I adopted because I wanted to do something to combat incarceration. I adopted because I wanted to do something about fear, low self-esteem, and brokenness. In the process I have learned what it means to help fill love tanks that have been completely emptied.

In the book, "The Five Love Languages of God" by Gary Chapman, he states:

> *"A teen who feels abandoned, rejected or abused will almost certainly struggle with self-worth, meaning and purpose. His or her love tank will be empty, and eventually the pain of feeling unloved will show up in the destructive behavior of the teenager."*

I agree that love should always be part of the answer, but education is important as well. Securing appropriate educational avenues for the youth who has spent his formative years in foster homes can be difficult. It is almost impossible to get a quality education when every three to six months a young person is being transferred from one home to another, having to adjust to another environment, and at the same time wondering when they will have to make another move.

This is not the reality for all kids in foster care, but it is the reality of too many kids in foster care. Every time a youth in foster care moves from one home to another, their life turns into what looks like a sheet of paper being torn to shreds. And then, before the pieces of the paper or their lives can be put back together, there is a move to another placement.

Amid it all, if a child is failing at securing math and reading scores that reach their grade level, they receive less respect than the student who is on point with their test scores. It's easy to look at people and determine that they are responsible for their circumstances. Many children in foster care have very little control over what happens in their lives.

As we all know, there are individuals who succeed despite their circumstances. I have several friends who have achieved unbelievable success after growing up under circumstances that were less than stellar. The difference in the kid who succeeds and the one that does not is the advantage of having a support system.

That support system can be a teacher, a counselor, a Pastor, or any person who is an encourager or edifier, someone who knows how to build up a young person emotionally and spiritually until they believe they really are somebody special.

In either of these cases, discrimination, bias, and racism is detrimental. Take for example, the young person who has been knocked down all their lives. Bias takes them further and further down; crushing their spirit until they look and feel like they're losing hope.

Some of these young people end up in juvenile detention. I know because I 've seen them there when I volunteered at DuPage County Juvenile Detention. Even for those young people who have intact self-esteem, bias can be detrimental because it's a reminder that they are different. Children in foster care must deal with this kind of ignorance on a regular basis.

My oldest adopted daughter is profoundly deaf. My oldest adopted son is deaf and mentally ill. He was three when he was adopted, and he is the product of a rape. His mother, who was fourteen years old and resided in a state-run facility, was either violated by a resident or a staff member. No one really knows. I was told that my son's mother was functioning intellectually at the level of a toddler. At the time the sexual assault took place, she was being tube fed, in diapers and bedridden.

One day, the staff at the facility noticed that my son's birth mother was experiencing some level of difficulty. They rushed her to the hospital and found out she was in labor. She had carried her/my son for seven months without notice and without prenatal care because no one knew she was pregnant until she got ready to deliver.

I made the decision to adopt when I was fifteen years old. That year my best friend got pregnant. Her mom was terribly angry about it and made her leave the house. She became a ward of the state and lived in several foster homes in less than a year. We recently had a conversation about her foster care placements.

I always thought that her placements were less than favorable, but she corrected me and said she didn't think her placements were bad at all. I did learn something else that I did not know. She said she walked away from foster care and never heard from DCFS or from any one of her social workers again.

Because I saw her placement as not being favorable, I decided that I would be responsible for taking at least one child out of foster care; that I would be responsible for filling a "love tank" that had been emptied by being in one placement after another.

As a foster parent, I was also able to get up close and personal with people and their ignorance or lack of knowledge. The biggest turn off for me as a foster parent was people's inability to be sensitive to the children who were living in my home. People would walk up to me, even in front of other people, and say, (right in front of the child), "Is this the one you have in foster care?" I still cringe just thinking about it.

No child, no matter what age, wants to be singled out as the foster child in front of a room full of people. Furthermore, any child who lived in my home became mine (if it was okay with them) no matter how long their stay was. I could usually measure that by whether they decided to call me Mom or not. At that point I felt like they had figuratively adopted me.

At my house we did not differentiate. None of our children were identified as foster children, adopted children or biological children unless it was necessary. By necessary I mean for example we're in the doctor's office and he assumes that the child and I share medical histories.

Today I will clarify for people which of my children are adopted and which are foster or biological when I am not in their presence because they are all grown up. However, in their presence, they are still just my kids. I mention it here in hopes that someone, somewhere will be motivated to foster and adopt as well.

In the past I have had people send Christmas cards and invitations that did not say Mr., Mrs., and family, but Mr. and Mrs and the name of our biological son only. And maybe it's just me but I see it as pure prejudice against adoption. I can't tell you how many people's lack of knowledge motivated them to ask me, "Why would you want to take care of somebody else's kids?" For those people who feel that way, sometimes there is no explanation that will satisfy them.

The Disabled Individual's Life Matters

For many years I believed my only motivation to adopt came from an experience that my best friend lived through as a teenager. It was my first experience with foster care and the Department of Children and Family Services.

This may have been my original motivation for adopting but after the adoptions took place, I realized as life moved forward, there were a lot of additional reasons why I wanted to adopt, some of which I mentioned earlier.

I also realized later that my motivation to adopt disabled children came from a different place altogether. I was very moved by the movie, "Of Mice and Men." I saw it when I was incredibly young, and it was the plight of one of the main characters that really impacted my life.

While connecting all the dots, I remember that it was just a year later. when I had a very moving and painful experience that I've carried with me for a lifetime. I was reminded of the experience recently while watching an episode of the now popular television show Investigative Discovery.

The episode I'm referring to took place during the 60's and was about a family who was physically disabled. They were involved in what was called the Freak Show at the circus. While watching the program, memories of a similar experience that I had as a child came flooding back to me.

They were memories of my visit to Riverview, the amusement park in Chicago that operated between 1904 and 1967. As my family and I walked around the park together for the first time, I was initially very excited about the lights, the people, the rides and all the things that tend to get adolescents excited at an amusement park.

Unfortunately, that excitement was short lived. It was 1965 and after going on a ride called the Bobs, a roller coaster that made me miserable, we passed a booth that had in bold writing at the top: FREAK SHOW.

I remember asking my mother about it. I don't remember her explanation exactly, but if I know my mother, and if she knew I was disturbed, she gave the best and most appropriate answer she could muster; and that I could be sure of.

Despite what she said, I was terribly saddened by the looks on the faces of those people who were standing on the outside of the curtain. My mother did tell me that people paid money to see this freak show and that there was more to see behind the curtain.

All I can tell you is I still remember the sadness on the faces of the people who were standing there on display. It was sadness like I had never seen before. I remember seeing a little person and a person who appeared to have what I now know might be an enlarged head because of hydrocephalus. There was another person whose face seemed to have large lesions with the skin hanging very low on the side of each jaw.

Even at my young age, I just couldn't believe it. I just didn't have the skills to express my deepest feelings about how wrong it all was; and how the freak show was such a horrible idea. I had thoughts like, "Who is forcing these people to do this?" and "Why are they doing this?" and "Who can help me make this stop?" I was devastated.

I have a younger cousin who has hydrocephalus and his mother, who is also my cousin, treats him with only tender, loving care. My mother again tried to assure me that the people were not as sad as I thought.

"Being in a freak show gives them an opportunity to make a living," she told me. And I was thinking, "How can I call the police or Heaven or someone and get every one of those people freed from this form of slavery that they are in?"

In my eyes, their lives mattered and what they were doing was not a good representation of that. It mattered on a level that should have required that they experience the same tender, loving care that my cousin would experience throughout his life, the same protection that is afforded to disabled people through the Americans with Disabilities Act.

And this, I believe with all the dots connected, is one of the reasons I adopted disabled children and the reason I've worked with disabled children and adults at least half of my adult life.

I love that today even young people are stepping up to the plate on behalf of disabled students. I repeatedly hear stories where young non-disabled students stand up for students who are disabled; students who have been bullied in their elementary or middle schools. I would like to share one of the best newspaper articles I have ever read:

Middle School Basketball Players See What's Happening in Stands Walk Off Court

"Three middle school basketball players recently came to the defense of a cheerleader with Down Syndrome who was being bullied by fans in the crowd. The incident happened at Lincoln Middle School, located in Kenosha, Wisconsin.

During the basketball game, Miles Rodriquez, Chase Vasquez and Scooter Terrun noticed fans bullying Desiree Andrews and the trio decided to defend their classmate, the Week reports. Chase Vasquez told TMJ4 in Milwaukee, "The kids in the audience were picking on D, so we all stepped forward."

After they noticed, more players gathered around to support Andrews, who was in the eighth grade. Rodriquez, who is 14, told Kenosha News, "We were mad. We didn't like that. We asked our sports director to talk to the people and tell them not to make fun of her."

The boys have befriended Andrews since the incident. They often walk her to class and now call the gymnasium, "Dee's House."

Andrews said the gesture was, "sweet, kind, awesome, amazing." Her father, Cliff Andrews, said that he was unable to choke back tears when he thanked the basketball players for their act of kindness.

"I was unable to choke back tears as I recant this beautifully sweet, kind, awesome and amazing act of kindness."

School spirit at Lincoln Middle School has increased following the event, with students focusing on inclusion and kindness, the New York Daily News report.

"It's not fair when other people get treated wrong, because we're not the same: God made us the same way." (Alex Groberman; The Week, TMJ4, Kenosha News, NY Daily News).

The Lives of
Deaf People Matter

My daughter was born deaf. She uses sign language to communicate. When she was 18 years old, she was able to get information about her biological family from the Department of Children and Family Services. I remember the night she came to my bedroom after reading the one-page commentary about her past. To her it felt like an assassination of her character and she wept openly.

The contents of the one-page paper said, in so many words, that there were three children that her mother and father could not care for. As we read together, it became clear that my daughter's grandmother stepped in to take her brother and sister but was unable to deal with my daughter's hearing impairment. With no other family members willing to take her in, my daughter became a ward of the state.

After reading the letter sent by the department, my daughter concluded that her biological family *did not* want her because she was deaf and *did* want her siblings because they were not. It was very difficult to convince her otherwise, but I'm my mother's daughter so I pulled out all stops.

I made it very clear that her father and I had chosen her; and that giving birth was different from adoption because in adoption you get to choose, while with a birth you just have to take whatever you get. She thought that was funny and she seemed to be coming around for a minute until the agony of it all hit her again.

"They didn't want me because I am deaf," she repeated through tears, sniffles and sign language. She got so upset that she started vomiting. I am tearful reliving it right now. I rocked her until she fell asleep. It was a kind of 'through the roof' sadness and it shook me to my core.

I told her we looked all over for a little girl who was deaf, which was true; and we wanted her to also be kind and funny. But when we couldn't find her in Illinois, we told the social worker to search in other states. I told her how happy we were when we heard that she was living in Ohio and waiting for a forever family.

I told her we couldn't have been happier when she became our daughter. And the truth is, that for every year that we've been together as mother and daughter, my love for her has grown stronger. In my eyes, when it comes to daughters, she is the cream of the crop.

Eric Smith

In 1996 Eric Smith, a 22-year-old African American deaf man was shot and killed by Forest View police officers on Interstate 55. Eric was my daughter's classmate throughout grammar school and high school. My family knew Eric very well.

A few years before, while Eric was attending Gallaudet College in Washington D.C., he left his apartment to flag down a police officer, because when he arrived home, he found that his apartment had been broken into. Around the same time, a police office in the area had been shot.

For some reason, Eric was mistakenly identified as the person who was the suspect in the shooting. Several police officers converged on Eric while he was standing on the sidewalk trying to flag down an officer to report a crime that had been committed against him. The D.C. officers beat him so badly that he spent three weeks in the hospital.

Eric was a six-foot one-inch wrestler, who in 1992 was named athlete of the year at the Illinois School for the Deaf. My guess is that when the officers saw this tall Black man with a wrestler's physique, screaming and communicating emphatically with his hands, they did not see a person trying to convey their innocence, but instead, saw him as a threat. They thought he looked threatening enough to be responsible for shooting an officer, moments earlier that day.

What they didn't know is that Eric was probably terrified, and that deaf people may scream louder because they can't hear how loud they're screaming. It is cultural, and when a deaf person is upset, their arms can seem like they're flailing violently (in the eyes of a hearing person) because they are communicating through 'sign' in a big way.

I have seen the response to an upset deaf person by police officers done right. My own son, who is deaf and diagnosed as borderline schizophrenic, had an explosive episode once while we were visiting the doctor's office.

He literally cleared the place. He got upset and started yelling, flailing his arms and knocking over chairs, and anything else that was in his way. The people in the room started leaving immediately. He was upset with me because my daughter had forgotten to bring the formula for my grandson, and I was giving her a hard time about it. When it was all said and done, he was probably right for thinking I was overreacting. We were at the health department and they had formula there.

When he started coming at me, my daughter, who is barely five feet tall, started jumping on him and hanging on to his neck trying to slow him down. When she started losing her ground, I had to pick up a chair to keep something between myself and my son, while at the same time trying to stay safe.

A nurse came into the room, and without knowing it, she started using the sign, "calm down." My son seemed to become mesmerized, either by the fact that she knew sign language or by the fact that she had the courage to come into the room to try and help.

For the most part, deaf people appreciate it when hearing people use sign language. They also appreciate warnings, advice and information from hearing people. The nurse encouraged me to leave the room. I swear this lady could have taken a job as a hostage negotiator. When she walked into that room, she took complete control.

When the police arrived, without any knowledge of how to communicate with a deaf individual, the officers had my son completely calm before he was taken to the hospital.

Unfortunately, years later, things did not go that well for Eric Smith and Forest View police officers. On April 9, 1996, Eric and his mother and grandmother were travelling on I-55 after leaving a counseling session for Eric. Eric got into a disagreement with his mother, and she decided to pull the car over on the shoulder to try to communicate better with him.

According to the news report, when the police arrived, Eric was very upset and did not comply when the officers gave him directives. First, he had no idea what they were saying, and his mother and grandmother could not help because they had never learned sign language.

The Forest View police officers who arrived on the scene said, "the 6-foot-one-inch, 270-pound college wrestler was difficult to apprehend," and as a result he was shot 6 times by officers, which resulted in his death.

Deaf lives matter. They matter more to me because I have three generations of deaf individuals in my family. My son and daughter are deaf; my grandson is hard of hearing and I have a great granddaughter who is also deaf.

The truth is that all lives matter. It depends on what you bring to the table. We "feel" because of our experiences. If you are African American and you have children, then Black lives will be your focus. If you are the parent, grandparent and great grandparent of deaf individuals and you're Black, well... you get my drift.

If you are the parent of someone who is LGBTQ, you will be more concerned than others about those in the LGBTQ community. If you are the parent, wife, son or daughter of a police officer, then your focus on what matters will be an overriding concern for police officers.

This book is in no way meant to take away from the "Black Lives Matter" movement. I applaud the movement and everyone who has poured so much energy into a movement that is making our world a better place.

Racial Profiling

What is racial profiling? What precipitates it and how is it perpetuated? Profiling, by definition, "has been conceptualized as the targeting of an individual based on race and not on criminal activity." *(Satzewich & Shaffir, 2009).*

According to the American Civil Liberties Union, "Racial profiling refers to the discriminatory practice by law enforcement officials of targeting individuals for suspicion of crime based on the individual's race, ethnicity, religion or national origin. Examples of racial profiling are the use of race to determine which drivers to stop for minor traffic violations, (commonly referred to as "driving while black or brown"). Some critics believe that the term "racial profiling" is synonymous with the term "racial discrimination."

Racial profiling is actually a term that cropped up in the last twenty years but has been a factor for African Americans or people of color since the end of slavery. I am reminded of the Pulitzer Prize winning novel by Harper Lee, which was later made into a movie entitled, "To Kill a Mockingbird."

Gregory Peck plays Atticus Finch who is a lawyer defending Tom Robinson, played by Brock Peters. Robinson has been accused of making passes at a young white girl in the community. Finch subsequently loses the case and before the night ends, he finds that Robinson has allegedly been killed trying to escape.

The movie is the focal point of what injustice has looked like for African Americans who are in the lower socioeconomic structure in this country. This novel is said to be read by more students than any other novel written on injustice.

Although this is a fictional story, there are a countless number of "real" stories; especially during the Jim Crow era, that took place when injustices and racial profiling against African Americans was so commonplace. For many years, while 'profiling' remained unnamed, racial injustice plagued people of color on a much more regular basis.

"Walking while brown" or "driving while Black" are a couple of nicknames or phrases used to describe situations where Africans Americans and Hispanics are "unconstitutionally criminalized" because of racial profiling. "Driving while Black" was taken from the term "driving while intoxicated" and was coined to mean if you're "driving while Black" you will be singled out by police and stopped without provocation.

In his New York Times bestseller, "Losing the Race: Self Sabotage in Black America," John McWhorter said, "A police officer can, quite reasonably, stop more young Black people, (especially males), than any other type of person without being racist at all."

"On the contrary, to do so is often the only logical way to effectively fight crime. But if this attention to minorities were unfair, the minorities checked would always come up empty-handed. But as we have seen, all too often, this is not the case. All of us know that, especially since the 1980's there has been a violent drug trade run by urban minority men." According to McWhorter, this would lead Black men in certain places to be more likely to be carrying drugs.

Despite McWhorter's claims, racial profiling derives from behaviors that have plagued the African American community since the post slavery decades after the Civil War. This could be a symptom of what Cronkite, in the book, "Criminal Justice Administration," calls the "Us" and "Them" mentality, where it's necessary to put someone else down so that we can feel better about ourselves.

Today, however, racial profiling encompasses a larger set of circumstances, one of which included Arizona's SB 1070 statute that was signed into law in 2010. Under SB 1070, Arizona law enforcement officers were required to stop anyone they believed was an illegal or undocumented immigrant.

If, when stopped, the individual is unable to process proof that they are a U.S. citizen, they could face six months in jail and have to pay a $500 fine. Their second infraction will be considered a felony. This phenomenon in Arizona has been given the name, "walking while brown."

After the September 11th terrorist attacks on the World Trade Center in New York, racial profiling would impact another group of people who would suffer greatly because of the behavior of a few. Because the Twin Towers were taken down by Al Qaeda terrorists, who happened to be Muslim, an all-out war was waged on the Muslim community because it seemed that the public could not separate the behavior of a few from the lives of innocent people.

"For example, more than 1,700 incidents of harassment, discrimination and violence against Arabs, Muslims and those thought to resemble those groups have been reported to organizations including the FBI, Federal Bureau of Investigation, the ACLU, American Civil Liberties Union, the Council of American-Arab Relations and the American Arab Anti-Discrimination Committee." *(Ramirez, Hoopes & Quinlin, 2003)*

After 9/11, Arab-Americans and Muslims have been asked to leave aircrafts because of suspicion from other passengers. There is an actual example of an Arab-American man who was part of President Bush's Secret Service detail who had an airline issue. According to the Secret Service, he was asked to leave the plane because the pilot questioned his credentials.

"Once seated on the plane, airline security personnel asked the agent to submit to additional security checks. After a delay of an hour and fifteen minutes – during which time the agent was questioned by the flight's pilot, airline officials and airport police. He was subsequently ordered to be removed from the flight despite offering to have the Secret Service confirm his identity."

"Ibrahim Hooper of the Council on American-Islamic Relations said, "the agent, who did not want to be identified, told him he felt he had been kicked off the Baltimore-to-Dallas flight because of his religion and ethnicity."(*"Muslim Secret Service Agent Removed from American Airlines Flight," by Douglas Kiker).*

In 2015 there were a couple of incidents that involved Muslim or Middle Eastern passengers on Southwest Airlines. In one incident, complaints were made by other passengers after hearing the Muslim passengers speaking

Arabic, according to NBC Philadelphia. Both men came to the United States from Palestine.

"The threshold for "see something, say something" is meant to apply to suspicious behavior, not personal prejudices against minorities engaging in non-suspicious behavior." The group's Chicago Executive Director, Ahmed Rehab of the Chicago Office of the Council on American-Islamic Relations, (CAIR), said in a statement.

As much as I am embarrassed to admit this, even I have experienced a certain level of discomfort after 9/11 while traveling on an airplane. When a group of men, who were all wearing turbans and communicating in a foreign language, boarded the plane I was on after 9/11, all I could see was one humongous red flag. And all I could think about was how the best decision I ever made in my life might be to deplane and save myself from being involved in a hijacking.

This embarrassing reaction might be related to my ignorance and/or lack of exposure to and experience with the Arab community. My response could also be a result of negative influence from peers or from the media.

As difficult as it is to admit my ignorance, I hope it frees someone else from feeling horrible about a temporary lapse in judgment. I hope it will motivate us all to learn more about cultures that we don't know much about. In the interim I took a position with a company whose staff were ninety-nine percent Arab American. In addition, there was one White person, one Hispanic person and one Black person who happened to be me. During that time, I learned a lot about Islam, gained more knowledge about the culture, learned a tiny bit of Arabic and as a bonus, made lifelong friends.

Racial profiling creates discord between the community and the police department. The practice breaks down relationships and hampers any means of being able to operate in a community-policing mode. Relationship is key, and when the relationship is broken down—between the police and the community—by feelings of disrespect and of being treated unfairly, the profiled individual will cease to cooperate or help police when help is needed.

This proves to be true whether the people profiled are African American, Hispanic, Asian Americans or Arabs who are Muslim. Information and intelligence are so vital to the police, the FBI, CIA, and Homeland Security. This makes it vitally important that these agencies establish great relationships with their community.

The department would probably be better able to fight crime by building relationships than profiling because then, there is a better chance they can get people to communicate with them about what is happening in their community, abroad or elsewhere.

"No data demonstrates either a general or a circumstantial correlation between race and crime. While a wealth of data exists regarding the number of persons arrested and convicted in this nation. there are inherent limitations in this data. The main limitation is that the data focuses on arrests and convictions, rather than on actual incidence or criminal conduct."

There are a wide range of feelings about racial profiling that cover a huge spectrum of attitudes and opinions. Slate magazine writer Michael Kinsley believes that profiling and affirmative action are the same thing.

"Racial profiling and affirmative action are analytically the same thing. When the police officers stop Black drivers or companies make extra efforts to hire Black employees, they are both giving certain individuals special treatment based on racial generalization. The only difference is that in one case, the special treatment is something bad and in the other case, it's something good."

Kinsley goes on to say that the police officer's need to fight crime is greater than having to worry about hurting the feelings of individuals. He believes that those people who gripe about racial profiling, in his words, need to get over it. He also believes that if we can avoid another 9/11 incident, it's worth it to make Arab men uncomfortable by singling them out at airport security checkpoints.

I guess in a perfect world, we could "weed out" those people, who are harboring the kind of hatred that makes them feel they have a license to act out in a negative manner toward another human being. Since we can't do that, we may need new laws to combat racial profiling.

In the book, "Losing the Race" McWhorter also says:

"There will always be bad cops. There are bad Black people and good black people, bad white people and good white people. Life isn't perfect. But just as one Black person's conduct cannot be interpreted as an indictment of the race, isolated incidents of excess from whites cannot be taken as evidence that the whole system is racist."

One only has to pick up the newspaper or read Internet news to see how many young Black men are being gunned down by members of today's police force: Michael Brown on August 9, 2014; Tamir Rice on November 22, 2014; Ronald "Ronnieman" Johnson on October 12, 2015; Philando Castile, Alto Sterling and Laquan McDonald who was shot and killed by officer Jason Van Dyke in Chicago – to name a few individuals who are loved and missed by family and friends.

Aside from "driving while Black" or "walking while brown," we can go back less than one hundred years and find documentation of racial profiling. In 1941, when the Japanese bombed Pearl Harbor, Americans were responsible for putting 120,000 Japanese people in internment camps to secure our nation.

It didn't matter that some of these individuals were Japanese American or that for some loyalty landed in the direction of the United States. At that time, the only criteria for taking these individuals away from their homes, and from everything else they were used to, was that they looked Japanese.

I have a friend who was in the military during World War II. I noticed that he occasionally made derogatory comments about Asian people. I wanted to point out to him that he really got my attention when he did that, so I asked him why he had so much resentment toward Japanese people.

"I fought in World War II and every time I see those slanted eyes, I still see the enemy," he said.

My response was, "You mean you've harbored that hatred for over 60 years?"

"I can't help it," he said.

It seems that living while Japanese can be a problem in some circles as well.

Because of this story, I was even more encouraged by the late Arizona Senator John McCain's mission to mend the relationship between Vietnam and the United States. This happened after he was a prisoner of war in a Vietnam prison for almost five years. McCain taught us all something about reaching across every aisle and accepting differences in all walks of life. He was a profile in courage, in the truest sense of the word.

In the end, there is nothing good that can come from racial profiling. America has recently proved that once again by separating immigrant children from their parents and housing them in cages.

America...America... God shed [your] grace on thee – and crown thy good with brotherhood from sea to shining sea.

Blue Lives Matter

"I know being a cop is hard. I know that sh*t's dangerous. I know it okay. But some jobs can't have bad apples. Some jobs, everybody gotta be good. Like pilots. Ya know. American Airlines can't be like, "Most of our pilots like to land. We just got a few bad apples that like to crash into mountains. Please bear with us."
-Chris Rock

I have worked and volunteered with several individuals in my community who have special needs of one kind or another. Most of these people require different kinds of support. As my record reflects, I have been a foster parent for the Department of Children and Family Services (DCFS).

I have worked with deaf children, deaf/blind children and adults, individuals who are HIV positive and or living with the AIDS virus; I have lived with and worked with individuals who are mentally ill, developmentally disabled and with individuals who are justice involved or who have been incarcerated.

I have also volunteered with victims of domestic violence and with perpetuators of domestic violence. I have worked with and volunteered my entire adult life with individuals in the homeless community and with seniors living with Alzheimer's-dementia and/or individuals in hospice at the end of their lives.

One thing that rings true in every one of these situations is that there are always a handful of people who should never hold a position with an organization that provides care for people who are deaf, blind, mentally ill, HIV positive, living with dementia, over the age of eighty, etc. I have worked and volunteered beside staff that should have never held an employment position in a prison, nursing home or a homeless shelter.

As a side note, and I feel like I need to clarify: Most of the people I volunteered with and worked side by side with were "all in" so to speak. The "all in" people are those people who have a heart for their community and a heart for the individuals they are serving.

For this reason, I am not referencing volunteers. In most volunteer situations, the individual who is volunteering has made a conscious decision to serve the individuals they are working with in a compassionate and loving manner. This makes a lot of sense because to volunteer is a choice.

As a volunteer myself, I have had an opportunity to work side by side with paid staff at a few organizations that served the community. A handful of people, who were employed with these companies were not all in. Some of them were there simply because they needed a job.

There were others who took positions for perhaps what they thought were the right reasons. When people come to the "service" table with inappropriate training and their own ideas of how things should be done, it's not enough to get them to treat the clientele they are serving in an appropriate manner.

I was shocked once to hear one staff person at a homeless shelter make negative and generalized comments about the people in the homeless community that the organization served. I choose not to repeat her comment because they would be hurtful to anyone in the homeless community who is reading this right now.

When I asked her why she chose to work with homeless people, she said she did it because she needed a job and that she couldn't wait until she was able to find work with a different company.

I have also worked beside individuals who served disabled children as well as senior citizens who lacked the sensitivity and compassion that these jobs require. My experience as a foster parent led me to meet a foster mother who took family photos while her two foster daughters sat by observing a family photo being taken without them.

The point I'm trying to make is this: Just because a person is working in a certain position doesn't mean that person is qualified or even a good fit for the position. I am sure this can ring true in almost every position where people are serving in their community and that includes the police department.

There are police officers who love what they do who are "all in" when it comes to their job. I know that because in addition to the positive experiences I have had with officers who have assisted me in the community, I also went to school with several police officers while working on my Master's degree in criminal social justice. It became my pleasure to get up close and personal with many of Chicago's finest.

One of my more interesting experiences (that was not so warm and fuzzy) was my interview with an officer who worked for the Justice Department. The officer freely admitted to me that people who commit crimes are the scum of the earth. She vehemently disagreed with me when I told her that people who are justice involved (like anyone else) should not be prejudged or lumped into one category. We went back and forth with our disagreements.

This officer told me that she worked with sex offenders and she admitted that she hated them. She told me she derived pleasure out of finding sex offenders out of their jurisdiction where she would have an opportunity to rough them up before taking them in.

I would tell her how wrong I thought she was, and she would tell me how wrong she thought my feelings were. Despite our differences, I hope each of us learned something from the other. The good news is we were both in a place where we were being educated and exposed to more experiences regarding criminal social justice.

This is where I want to give a shout out to the Chicago Police Department and the United States Justice Department for supporting their officers in training through higher education. Just as education, exposure and experience can help bridge the gap between differences in our community, the same can be true for "blue lives" as well.

I think it would be great if part of an officer's training required them to log in several volunteer hours in a prison, detention center or mental health facility. I also believe if officers are required to log in volunteer hours as part of their training, they would have more empathy for individuals they have minimal experience with.

If they are not volunteering in a prison or detention center, I think it would be just as effective for them to volunteer in homeless shelters, centers that work with women of domestic violence or with people who are disabled or dealing with mental health issues.

As I mentioned before, (CPD) the Chicago Police Department is on board with higher education for their officers and has a program where the department pays for a master's degree for officers as long as they keep their grades up. For example, according to the officers that I went to school with, CPD pays 100% for a grade of "A" and the amount of what they pay goes down as the grade goes down. In other words, there is less financial support for a grade of B and even less for a grade of C.

About three quarters of the students in the Criminal Social Justice program at Lewis University were Chicago police officers. This is only my visual statistic. Most of them felt good about the fact that the department saw education as being essential for them to do a better job on the street.

I know that because as an undergraduate Communications-Journalism major, I have a tendency to interview almost everyone I meet. One time when a friend introduced me to her friend from out of town, the friend said I didn't know I was going to be meeting Oprah. And I wanted to say – "You know I was supposed to be Oprah and she somehow stole my job and my money." I am literally laughing out loud as I type this.

There are many police officers on the force that are doing a fantastic job. I have gone to school with, worked with and had service provided by officers who I would rate as top notch. However, police officers, just like many others who work in service positions, can have multiple issues that have no place in the police department or in the community where those officers are working.

We all know that some officers come to the table with issues of racism, bias, low self-esteem and substance abuse issues, which can exacerbate excessive force and lead to criminal behavior by these police officers.

I think that as we consider the life of the police officer, we must make sure that we are not guilty of doing the same thing that some of them are doing in our community. We must make sure that we are not behaving like some of them by generalizing or lumping all of them into a single category, and/or showing prejudice or discriminatory behavior towards them. We have to keep in mind that there is good and bad in every profession.

We need to also remember that police officers have families who want them to return home after a day of work just like we want our Black and Brown sons and daughters to come home to us without falling prey to the unreasonable shooting incidents that have taken place in our communities.

I believe the gap between the police and the community can be bridged and I believe there are multiple layers of things that are needed. In addition to those things that "the powers that be" decide, I think we need to have officers volunteer in areas where they have little or no experience. People disagree with me, but I believe we need to bring back community policing which will give officers more exposure and experience in the communities they work in.

It is also imperative that the blue code of silence be eradicated completely and that those who have inappropriate behavior in their positions be removed from those positions sooner rather than later.

LGBTQ Lives Matter

*"Our culture has accepted two huge lies. The first is that
if you disagree with someone's lifestyle, you must fear or hate
them. The second is that, to love someone means you agree
with everything they believe, say or do. Both are nonsense.
you don't have to compromise convictions to be
compassionate." Dave Chappelle*

In the book, "I Was Born This Way," by Archbishop Carl Bean, he mentions a congregant who asked, "Reverend, does God hate me because I'm a lesbian... or transgendered... or bisexual.... Or black or poor... or sick with disease?"

"No, my children: It is not God who causes us to live as outcasts. In their quest for power and position, human beings create categories to elevate themselves and belittle others. If we accept the world's scorn, we grow weak. If we accept God's love, we grow strong. I promise this. I know this. My life is a testimony to one statement and one statement only – God is love and love is for everyone."

My adopted son is black, deaf, mentally ill and gay. Fortunately for him, his world of silence keeps him safe from most of the pain and ridicule inflicted by those who disagree with his sexual orientation. But for others in the LGBTQ community, the confusion, frustration and external condemnation can be tantamount to feeling like a cancelled stamp in the post office of life; or so I've been told.

George Valentia of the Trevor Project Suicide Hotline noted gay and lesbian people are three times more likely to attempt suicide, and every five hours an LGBTQ teen takes his or her life. According to Valentia, for every teen who takes their life, 20 more make an attempt.

One of the top five reasons teens call the hotline is for religious issues. "they feel there's no place for them and God," Valentia said.

In his book, "I Was Born This Way," Archbishop Carl Bean, who is openly gay, reassured a church group once in this way:

"Jesus is all inclusion, not exclusion. His simple but radical outlook as a rabbi of love was simply that love is available to all. He was a Jew, but his ministry went far beyond Jewish culture or religion. He hung out with outcasts. He nursed the sick, the blind and the insane... The notion that Jesus would exclude same-sex attracted humans from his all-inclusive grace went against the very essence of his miraculously loving nature."

Archbishop Bean then referenced Romans Chapter 8, Verse 38. "For I am persuaded that neither death nor life, nor angels, nor principalities, nor powers, nor things present nor things to come, nor height nor depth, nor any other created thing, shall be able to separate us from the love of God which is in Christ Jesus our Lord.

When New Hampshire priest Dean Robinson was elected Bishop of the Episcopal Church of the United States of America in 2003, he accepted the honor wearing a bulletproof vest. This kind of preventative measure taken by an openly gay priest at his ordination speaks volumes about where many Christians and non-Christians alike stand regarding LGBTQ individuals.

The Catholic Church teaches, "Basing itself on sacred scripture, which presents [same-sex] acts as acts of grave depravity, tradition has always declared that [same-sex] acts are intrinsically disordered. They are contrary to natural law [and] under no circumstances can they be approved" (*Catechism of the Catholic Church 2357*).

A Personal Thank You

Thank you, Fr. James Martin Sr., consultant to the Vatican's Secretariat for Communications and author of "Building a Bridge", for your efforts to bridge the gap between the LGBTQ community and the Catholic Church. Your courage has given me strength to stand up for what I believe in and I applaud you.

Many Christians outside the Catholic Church also condemn same-sex activity and use certain scriptures in the Bible to reinforce their attitude and beliefs.

In the film, "For the Bible Tells Me So," an American documentary about homosexuality and the Bible, producer Daniel Karslake points out the names of several organizations that believe that sexual orientation is not a choice, and that it cannot be changed through the method of reparative therapy. These organizations include:

The American Medical Association, The American Psychiatric Association, The American Psychological

Association, The National Association of Social Workers and The American Academy of Pediatrics.

Bishop Desmond Tutu, South African Cleric, Nobel Prize recipient and champion in the fight against AIDS, poverty, racism and homophobia, believes that the Bible speaks in the idiom of that time. Tutu further equates homophobia with apartheid, a form of legal racial segregation that took place in South Africa from 1948 to 1994. The use of certain words can be used to segregate the gay and straight community as well.

On June 12, 2016, our nation recently suffered a great loss and it took place at a bar in Miami that was named Pulse; in honor of the bar owner's brother, who died from complications due to AIDS.

A gunman walked into the bar and when he finished shooting, forty-nine people had been killed and another fifty had been injured.

Pulse is a gay bar and, according to police, the shooter's Dad said his son's behavior had resulted in seeing two gay men on the street showing affection toward one another.

After the shooting, Fox News intern Patience Carter, as part of her healing process, wrote a beautiful poem:

"The guilt of feeling grateful to be alive is heavy.
Wanting to smile about surviving but not sure the
people around you are ready.
As the world mourns the victims killed and viciously slain.
I feel guilty about screaming about my legs in pain
because I could feel nothing.
Like the other forty-nine who weren't so lucky to feel
this pain of mine.
I never thought in a million years that this could happen.
I never thought in a million years that my eyes could
witness something so tragic.

Looking at the souls leaving the of bodies of individuals.
Looking at the killer's machine gun throughout my
right peripheral.
Looking at the blood and debris covered on everyone's faces.
Looking at the gunman's feet under the stall as he paces.
The guilt of feeling lucky to be alive is heavy.
It's like the weight of the ocean's walls crushing
uncontrolled by levies.
Life being dragged through the grass with a shattered
leg and thrown on the back seat of a Chevy.
It's like being rushed to the hospital and being told
you're going to make it.
When you've laid beside individuals, whose lives are
brutally taken,
The guilt of being alive is heavy."

Patience Carter
May we never forget...

The AIDS Ride

In 2001 I participated in the Tanqueray Heartland AIDS Ride to raise money for HIV research. More than 1,500 riders biked from St. Paul, Minnesota to Montrose Harbor in Chicago, covering a grand total of more than 500 miles. According to rider Karen Hawkins, "the 1,500 riders and roughly 400 crew members raised 5.7 million.

Our group was extremely diverse. We rode 1,500 strong together with Black people, white people, Hispanics, Asians, LGBTQ individuals, straight people and with many participants who were HIV positive.

For the most part, it was a great time but there were a couple of negative incidents that were a little surprising and stand out in my mind. Most of the towns we rode through gave us grand receptions, which included welcome signs, balloons, bottled water, etc. But there was one town whose reception I was totally unprepared for.

When we rode through this town, there were signs that read, "Go Home Gays," "Gays Get Out!" — as well as other signs of the same nature. I was aghast! Call me naïve. I do know on some level people can be cruel, but I'm still thrown off when I witness this kind of cruel behavior first-hand and in person.

On the last leg of the ride, with more than 50 miles to go, we were rolling through another rural area in Illinois when I rode up to a café. A few of my fellow riders, who were leaving, encouraged me to stop in. They assured me that the restaurant was full of church women and according to my comrades, "the women were a delightful bunch."

"They're so excited about what we're doing," another rider said.

I was full of excitement and anticipation when I entered the establishment. Because of the rural area we were riding in, I wasn't surprised that the entire group of senior aged women were white. However, I was surprised at their response when I walked through the door.

If the place had had a heartbeat, it would have stopped when I walked into the room, the same way everything seemed to stop the minute I stepped through the door. Everything stopped – talking, movement, etc. If I hadn't known better, I would have thought that everyone in that group of approximately 20 women had stopped breathing. I felt very uncomfortable and confused. I walked to the counter and asked the waitress behind the counter where I could find the restroom. It wasn't that I needed to use the restroom, I just didn't know what else to do. This was the place where just a few minutes ago someone had told me that I could expect a great reception when I entered. There was nothing great about it.

Without looking at me and without uttering a mumbling word, the woman responded to my request by pointing in the direction at the back of the building. When I finally escaped behind the closed door, I only wanted to weep. My spirit was crushed. All the 'feel good' hormones, endorphins and serotonin that had been operating in full gear because of all the riding, had dissipated.

I began to ask myself, "Do I deserve to be treated as if I have leprosy?" Wasn't I engaging in the same 'good will' that the ladies who entered the restaurant before me were?" Maybe I was overreacting. Perhaps I had merely caught the women off guard, and it would take them a little longer to adjust because of their lack of experience with people who were different.

I wonder what their response would have been if these church women, who apparently had problems with individuals who were different, had known that my comrades who entered before me were all gay.

When I left the restroom, I felt their eyes boring down on me. "Have a nice day," I said, as I was leaving, without really making eye contact with anyone.

No response.

As I continued my ride alone with the 1,500 or so other riders ahead of me, I heard what sounded like a large vehicle coming up behind me. I looked in the rearview mirror on my ten-speed and saw an 18-wheeler approaching. I inhaled and then exhaled heavily. I prepared for the worst. I had already received negative reception in this town, so I was feeling very unwanted and alone – without another rider in sight.

I looked around me to find that yes... aside from the truck, I was very alone. There was no other sign of life ahead of me or behind me. As the truck approached, I could see the driver was a white male in his 30's. I was wearing my AIDS ride biking shirt as my only visible sign of identification.

The trucker started blowing his horn, which scared me at first and then I saw his face in my mirror. He had a million-dollar smile as he continued blowing his horn and giving me a thumbs up at the same time.

I weep whenever I remember. It was one of the best moments of my life. There are two very popular sayings in the Black community and they are, "God will show up and show out," and "He (God) always has a ram in the bush," which in both cases means – He will never let you down.

I was feeling crushed when I left that café, and when that 18-wheeler came barreling down the road, I prepared myself for the worst, for another crushing blow. But lo and behold, this trucker became God's "ram in the bush." To say he made me feel lifted up and revitalized would be an understatement: The feelings I had were much too deep for words. In a matter of minutes, that trucker's kindness had restored my faith in mankind.

My tent mate on the AIDS ride summed up the experience in a family Christmas card when she wrote:

"I said 'yes' to a rather unique challenge this last year, signing up for the Heartland AIDS Ride, A six-day, 500-mile bike ride from the Twin Cities to Chicago. Feeling prompted to 'move out of my comfort zone' I embarked on what became a journey of unbelievable kindness and joy... and it changed my life. Self-doubt and fear ebbed away in the light of encouragement and support I found; wounded healers all around me demonstrated to me what love and greatness were all about.

As for me, that trucker played a huge role in being a part of that love and greatness. My tent mate continued:

"Our world is broken, and we may still struggle to move forward after 9/11, but I will always remember the summer of 2001 when my entire planet seemed friendly, where trust prevailed and differences took a back seat to a larger denominator…a conspiracy of kindness, if you will…where team captains didn't hesitate to put themselves in harm's way to protect their members and strangers gave away signed checks to make sure riders met their pledge totals. It was a summer when the very hills clapped for joy and the gravel beneath our tires offered no resistance. Even the rocks cried out! And I will never forget it."

As my tent mate so eloquently expressed, the 2001 Heartland AIDS ride was the crème de la crème of positive experiences. We were all so different and yet connected on so many levels and in so many ways. I thank God for allowing me to end my ride the same way I started it; wrapped in a bundle of inspiration, friendship, kindness and love. I too, will never forget it.

Racism Matters

"There is no vaccine for racism…
we have to do the work."
Kamala Harris,
Vice President of the United States of America

One day while having brunch with a white girlfriend of mine, we started having a conversation about racism and hate groups. I told her about my visits to the white supremacy site StormFront.com. She assured me that she would never be able to visit such a site and thought it might be in my best interest to discontinue my visits. Her feeling was that these people had nothing to do with our real world; that these people operate in a vacuum, so to speak.

I found her feelings very interesting but was glad to be sharing with her. She tried to assure me that the people on the website were a bunch of radicals and not the same people that I would meet in my everyday life. She really thought I was off the mark.

The truth is—they are the same people; the same people that I have worked next to; the same people that have no regard for me as a human being when they forced me out of jobs or refused to hire me. It reminds me of the supervisor who told me that he could not eat his lunch out of a bag when I returned to the office with his lunch (after taking my lunch time to go get his) and placed it on his desk.

This is the same guy who stayed at a Christmas party on another floor with the rest of the office staff while I stayed and manned the phones. The same guy, who didn't say, when I got ready to quit that day. "Oh, I didn't know you hadn't had a chance to attend the party or even have lunch, or even take a bathroom break." The truth is he didn't care.

And again, I am reminded of another supervisor, who in front of a room full of people at a staff meeting decided that it was important for me to know that a monkey could do my job. I guess because he didn't get a reaction from me, he decided he would have to repeat himself a little later on in the meeting.

The point is that both of these white men had no regard for me as a human being and the more time I spent on the white supremacy website, the more I realized how prevalent the hate, animosity and hostility is in my everyday life.

Initially my friend tried to argue. I assured her that I had seen it plain as day and regularly throughout my entire life. I could look into her eyes and see the hurt and disappointment she felt, not just for me, but also for every individual in a minority group who is marginalized by racism. I knew her feelings were genuine.

It's easy for white people and some African Americans to accuse Black people of whining. In his book, "What's Race Got to Do With It?" Larry Elder calls for an end to "bitching, moaning and whining," by the African American community. As I stated earlier, I can support this premise, especially when it comes to people who use racism as an excuse for moving through life and living a mediocre existence, but on the other hand, racism's prevalence matters.

Yes, Mr. Elder, I can stop moaning and groaning when I get over the pain of being treated as if I'm less than. What about the kids whose parents did not think they were the eighth wonder of the world? Those kids whose self-worth and self-esteem has already been compromised.

I agree that that is still no excuse for whining, but when you arrive at the table and your love tank is empty; when you have not had any positive reinforcement throughout your entire life, racism becomes the additional pain and when it's piled on, it can cut you like a knife.

Does it really help to "suck it up" or ignore the hatred that still brews because of racism? Will ignoring it make it go away? I can ignore an injury I have gotten while running. I can run five miles through knee pain and by the time I get to what's called the "second wind," (the time when running becomes effortless), it's as if the pain does not exist anymore.

I suppose you could use the same formula for racism. The problem with racism, just like having a running injury is this: You feel the pain, you ignore it, and after some time, it might dissipate. However, if you don't address it, it comes back; just like the pain of racism, and each time the injury becomes more debilitating.

Let me explain by using an example: I recently volunteered at a baseball game. It was not your average baseball game. It's called beep baseball. It was a tournament where six blind teams came together in the Chicagoland area to compete for first prize for their team. All the teams were racially diverse, and all the volunteers were white. The team members were legally blind, and the only sighted players were the pitcher and the catcher.

Even though all the players were legally blind, some of them had a little more sight than others. Because of this, all the players were required to wear blindfolds as a way to level the playing field, so to speak.

Keeping in line with the name of the game, "beep baseball," the baseballs and the bases beeped. Spectators remained quiet during the runs so that the players would be able to hear the beeping base. Each time a player went up to bat he or she would have to listen for the sound of the ball to make contact with the bat.

The base, which beeped as well, was turned on immediately after the ball was hit and the player would run in the direction of the beeping base. Several volunteers were on the field to walk the player back home after they scored a point.

Because most players were very experienced, many of them took a straight line to the base instead of weaving in and out of the base line. There were also sighted volunteers on the field to make sure all outfield players got back on point after the hitter's ball was retrieved.

All the volunteers at the game were white and it was easy to see and feel the love and camaraderie that existed between the players and those people that were helping to make everything happen. It gave me a sense that everything was alright with the world. Being able to see such diversity in a group of people who were all in one place with everyone working together to reach a common goal was more than heartwarming.

It was like jogging with an injury and just forgetting about it. It made me temporarily forget the pain of racism and put me in the mode of the "runner's second wind:"

floating along effortlessly without a care in the world. When the run is over and when the game is over, reality sets in. The pain from the injury returns and just like the pain of racism, it begins to rear its ugly head again.

Linn Washington, Jr, a columnist for the Philadelphia Tribune, wrote this in an article entitled, Racism in America and Other Uncomfortable Facts: "The chronic inability of America to really address racism has corroded its lofty promises since before the drafting of the U.S. Constitution in Philadelphia over 200 years ago." He went on to say, "Forty years ago, the introduction of the Kerner Commission report noted white Americans "never fully understood what [Blacks] can never forget'—the role of white institutions in sustaining America's racially discriminatory society."

"It may surprise some, but Blacks want to move beyond racism also. Blacks have always wanted to move beyond, but racism blocks advance." Says Washington.

I agree with Washington. You can say what you want about Black folks being whiners, but racism does block advance. Not only does it block advance, but it can also be an unreasonable imposition for the person that it's directed at.

Take former Vice President Dick Cheney, who was addressed by CIA Director Leon Panetta in an AP news article. Panetta says former Vice President Dick Cheney's criticism of the Obama Administration's approach to terrorism almost suggests, "He's wishing that this country would be attacked again, in order to make his point." (*AP News*)

This is just one of the last in a stream of attacks that Cheney made against the Obama Administration. The most interesting part about all of this is that the public heard very little from Cheney for the eight years he was sitting vice president.

After that, he couldn't sit still because of what seemed like a burning desire to discredit President Barack Obama. What could really be the problem? Let me speculate here for a minute. There are some things that are going to happen in this country that are just going to bring the racism that's in some people, out! I pray I am wrong about Dick Cheney and that it really was not his desire to bring down the first Black president of the United States of America.

But for those people who are racist, I compare their racist behavior to the stress that brings on a heart attack. The pressure just keeps building and building until the heart attack ensues. The person starts out calm, they attend a secret white supremacy meeting; they get a username for the hate website; they move around operating in a spirit of tolerance for as long as it is possible. Then suddenly...boom!

Something earth shattering happens like, let's see, a Black man is elected president of these United States. Just like the heart attack, where the blood pressure is totally out of control, the racist (with his or her hateful behavior), works feverishly to interrupt or impede progress that would ultimately be positive.

This puts me immediately in the mind of President Donald Trump's running conspiracy theory that Barack Obama was not born in the United States. After Obama became president, Trump finally reluctantly admitted that the former president was in fact born here. I cannot say for sure if Trump's obsession with bringing Obama down had more to do with racism or if it had more to do with the fact that he is extremely envious and jealous of Obama.

I can't help but think of the Bible story of Saul and David and Saul's obsessive pursuit of David to kill him. The Bible tells us that when David returned from a war that Saul had him lead, "the women came out of all the cities of Israel singing and dancing, to meet King Saul, playing songs of joy on timbrels. The women sang as they played, and said, "Saul has killed his thousands, and David his ten thousand… And Saul was jealous and did not trust David from that day on."

There are a couple of correlations between Saul and Trump. Neither of them could get over the fact that there wasn't any way they could measure up at trying to be the person they were directing their jealousy, envy or bad feelings toward. The correlation between David and Obama is they were or are competent in their positions and did not feel any threat from anyone.

In both cases, Obama never publicly showed anger toward Trump's relentless bad behavior. The same holds true for David. Saul pursued David relentlessly to kill him because of his jealously but when David had Saul in a position to take his life, he did not do it because after all the things Saul had put him through, he was not angry.

How do we remove the figurative shackles of the racist? In the words of Donnie McClurkin on his soundtrack, "We Fall Down," there are repetitive lyrics that say: "We fall down but we get up… We get back up again, get back up again," until our impeded progress is no longer blocked. I get exhausted writing about it.

Imagine being the target of someone's relentless racism and even their envious behavior on a regular basis. Is it just me, or was our former president, Barack Obama, up against more than any other president has ever had to endure? Thank you, President Obama for "getting back up again" and again.

Makes me have a Peter, Paul and Mary moment: "If I had a hammer, I'd hammer [this fact] in the morning, in the evening and all over this world. If I had a bell, I'd ring it in the morning, in the evening and all over this world." It would be the same if I had a song to sing, "I'd sing it in the morning, evening and all over this land." I don't have a hammer, bell or song, but I've got a book to write and the goal is for as many people as possible to read it, feel it and digest it. Lord I can't breathe until Black Lives Matter. I can't breathe until "All Lives Matter."

Storm Front is a white supremacist website that began as an online bulletin board system in the 1990's. The website's slogan is "White Pride World Wide." It was established as a website in 1996 by Don Black who is a former Ku Klux Klan member and a white supremacist. It was "the Web's first major racial hate site." *(www.civilrights.org)*

A StormFront.com member named Rob had these questions posed by someone visiting the Website: "Do you really hate Black people and how do you feel about Martin Luther King?"

"I personally do not hate all Negroes. I have no problem with the ones in Africa or Jamaica or in other Black countries where they belong. I know Negroes were brought here as slaves. All I can say on that is that I didn't bring them here [but] I am just trying to figure out a way to send them back!" As for the Martin Luther King thing, I could care less one way or the other about it. As far as I'm concerned, he is just another dead [expletive]. At least the dead ones can't try to move into white neighborhoods."

Jason, another StormFront.com forum member, answered the same question:

"The answer to your question, "Do I really hate Black people is this: Yes, in fact I do really hate them. Regarding Martin Luther King, I hate him because he was a dirt bag and every year in school, we spent time learning about how great he was."

Ole dixie88, another StormFront.com forum member from southwest Virginia, explains Black culture: "Greetings brothers and sisters! After reading the forums for several months, I finally registered with hopes to become a productive member of the fine community here. Which brings me to my question. What exactly is Black Culture? What have these people ever contributed to society on their own? It seems to me that no matter where they go, destruction, murder, rape, and a general sense of stupidity follows right behind them. Why do we even have Black history month? I don't believe that they, as a people, have done anything productive throughout the history of humankind. Am I missing something here?"

Whitebread, in Schuylkill County, Pennsylvania, "where the illegals know their place," also says: "No one argues there are criminals in every race. However, Negroes are responsible for massive amounts of crime in this country... lots of it interracial. Not just on Whites, but on Asians also. No...crime will not come to a screeching halt, but we could take back our cities and slums that have been ghettoized and ruined after they are gone. And we won't have to worry as much about our women getting raped by a Negro who wants to stick it to Whitey."

Whitebread continues,..."think of the tax dollars we could save trying to lift Negroes up through government and self-help programs, out of their pathetic self-pity. "White man be keepin' me down lifestyles could be used to improve our schools drastically and help White children flourish, instead of them [white kids] being trapped in a school where the standards have been lowered so much for the lower IQ non-Whites that they are cheated out of real education."

Visiting the Stormfront site was quite overwhelming. When I exited the page, my mind was flooded with all kinds of thoughts. My first thought being, once again, that the thoughts and feelings of the Stormfront members are not taking place in a vacuum. Some of these individuals are on our police forces, members of Congress, on Wall Street, in doctor's offices, hospitals, CEOs of major companies, etc.

I'm left wondering how these people can legally spew such hate. How many of these hateful people are there in our world? It takes me back to a question another White friend asked not long ago. And she was very sincere when she asked, "Do you still think racism exists?

I wanted to shout it from the mountaintops! "Yes, yes, yes!!! And racist individuals have places where they can go and share these hateful ideas on social media." One other post that stood out to me on Stormfront was this one: "Obama will never rule the land of the Ku Klux Klan."

This is a perfect example, in my opinion, of freedom of speech gone too far. I agree with Alisyn Camerota, morning anchor on CNN, when she said, "Inflammatory words lead to hostility, which leads to violent actions." With these words in mind, this site and others like it need to be shut down... and much sooner than later.

In the documentary, "The Last White Knight," Director Paul Saltzman interviews killer and Klansman Byron De La Beck. During the interview he asks De La Beck if he is still a Klansman. De La Beck says, "Just like a Christian accepts Jesus Christ for life, a Klansman accepts being a Klansman for life."

De La Beck admitted to Saltzman that his mother was an alcoholic who occasionally tried to shoot him when he was a kid. He also admitted that he was afraid of his father and thought "his father thrashed him more than he should have been thrashed."

In my opinion, I've said it before and I'll say it again: In order to combat crime, we must be vigilant about combating child abuse. There are no statistics available, but I would be willing to bet that many of the white supremacists that have lived lives spewing hate have grown up in abusive and dysfunctional environments.

It is my criminal justice background, my work in foster care, my work with victims of domestic violence, perpetrators of domestic violence, my work with individuals who are justice involved, substance users or with those who are mentally ill that leads me to believe that hurt people hurt people.

There is a bit of good news that, despite De La Beck's 50 years of hateful feelings and behavior, he is quoted as saying, "My children do not take part in the Klan and do not feel the way I do."

All I can say is, "Thank God!"

"The number of hate groups operating in the United States continued to rise in 2008 and has grown by 54 percent since 2000; an increase fueled last year by immigration fears, a failing economy and the successful campaign of Barack Obama [in 2008]," according to the Southern Poverty Law Center (SPLC).

The SPLC identified 926 hate groups active in 2008, up more than 4 percent from the 888 groups in 2007, and far above the 602 groups documented in 2000. In 2018 the SPLC tracked 1020 hate groups across the U.S.

And... Racism Hurts

Hail to Keith Olbermann, former host of "Countdown with Keith Olbermann" on MSNBC. Keith Olbermann is one of the most "real" white people I've never met and there's a toss-up between Rush Limbaugh and Dick Cheney for being the most openly biased individuals I've never met.

I followed Olbermann on MSNBC because of his integrity and sincerity. These attributes overshadowed his celebrity. He spoke the truth and he did it with accuracy. Whenever he spoke that truth, I could always see his heart; a heart that seemed to be filled with intolerance for unfairness, prejudice and most of all, racism.

People may not always agree with Olbermann, but they must respect him for his authenticity and for speaking the truth for many of us, unlike some other pundits who refused to do so. I don't think I heard any other commentators utter the word racism before Olbermann.

However, today I have to give a shout out to the CNN commentators and reporters who have been on point on the subject of racism. In addition to Allisyn Camerota, John Berman and Abbey Phillip, the rest of the CNN commentators and reporters have been showing up and showing out on the racial justice platform; calling it like they see it and telling it like it is. I love you guys! But Chris Cuomo and Don Lemon, you are my all-time favorites.

Thinking of the racism or no racism conundrum reminds me of my mother who would never utter the word sex when my sister and I were kids. I wonder if she thought feelings about sex would never materialize if she just never said the word. I guess my mother thought of sex the way America thinks of racism. If we just ignore it and refrain from using the word, it will just go away. My hat is off to Keith Olbermann who stood in stark contrast years ago to this backward way of thinking.

Racism is in fact alive and well. We are still confronted with it, along with hatred and intolerance. Today there are still websites that are run by white supremacy groups that continue to spew hatred at every turn.

But just when I thought I would not be able to explain the racist who didn't know he was a racist, a Louisiana man by the name of Bardwell brought it home for me. After he refused to give an interracial couple a marriage license, he said, "I'm not a racist. I just don't believe in mixing races that way."

Bardwell told the Associated Press, "I have piles of Black friends. The come to my home, I marry them, they use my bathroom; I treat them like everyone else," he said.

Oh my gosh. What are the qualifications for becoming a Justice of the Peace? The ignorance on this front is absolutely appalling; the idea that it was made public is even more mind-boggling. As I reread what I've written here, I realize the reader may think I am being a little tough on Bardwell.

So, let me say this, "You say you 'have a pile of Black friends.'" My suggestion would be for you to get a few piles more. But with your next pile, please take the time to really get to know more about them, their culture and their hearts.

Washington University

A friend of mine told me one of his daughters, who is white and attends Washington University in St. Louis, told him that he was a racist when he cautioned her about the neighborhoods surrounding the Washington University campus. Her immediate response to his cautious behavior about the neighborhoods that were predominantly Black was, "Dad, you're such a racist. You're just behaving that way because there are Black people in the area."

Of course, my white friend was offended by the accusation. He doesn't consider himself to be a racist. He has a Black friend for crying out loud; at least one that I'm aware of, and that would be me.

Dad has, on the other hand, been very honest about admitting the superiority challenge of having white privilege. What this can translate into is: "I don't mean to make you feel bad; I'm really not a racist but I am a cut above." So, inevitably what will happen as a result is you get called out on the carpet by your children.

When you hear these words, "Dad, you're a racist, or even, "Mom, that's racist." Evaluate and reevaluate, and if you really feel like you want to be in line with making the world a better place for generations to come, stop it in its ugly tracks. If you don't, this is the kind of thing that can happen. You get caught up and eventually the truth will come out, quite possibly with the wrong people and in a much more uncomfortable scenario. And let all of this compute no matter what color you are.

The Foster Parents

My adopted daughter lived with a white family and her foster parents were at an age where they had grown children. They had been doing foster care for many years. They seemed to have a very close relationship with our future daughter when we met the family. In my opinion, they were wonderful, loving people. They had taken children into their home from all walks of life.

My daughter was Black and profoundly deaf. She had been in foster care for three years when our family met her. She was extremely delayed as a result of missing so much communication.

While residing with the Smith's (not their real names), my daughter was placed in a school that did not recognize the "total communication" philosophy. This philosophy teaches children to vocalize and use words to the best of their ability—using speech therapy—while using sign language at the same time to communicate.

My daughter never benefitted from total communication, not at school or at home because the family never learned to use sign language. She was enrolled in a school with hearing children who verbalized to communicate. The Smiths believed that familial gestures used in the home compensated enough for the seven-year-old deaf child that they had taken in at age four.

I am sure this family provided what they thought was best for my daughter while she resided with them in foster care. I do want to point something out that was very confusing to me; something that kind of indirectly relates to my daughter.

We continued to stay in contact with the family after the adoption was final. Three or four years later the foster mother told me—very innocently, I might add—that when her white adopted daughter announced that she was marrying a Black man, the foster dad hit the ceiling. In other words, he was not happy.

This is where I got concerned and confused. Mr. Smith allowed a Black child to live in his home for four years and then in the next breath decided that an older Black adult male was not a desirable choice for his adopted white daughter. What if my now adopted daughter was still living with you when you hit that ceiling? How do you think that would have made her feel?

Bosom Buddies

I'm reminded of a couple of remarkably close friends I had in college. There were three of us who hung out together all the time. Both friends were white. We called ourselves "The Mod Squad" which is a spin off from an 80's TV show where three cops, two white one Black, were on a sitcom for five seasons.

The three of us were thick as thieves. We were bosom buddies: We were very close, intimate friends who always had each other's backs and with whom we shared everything. We were the Mod Squad.

Sharon, not her real name, was from a medium sized city and Stan, not his real name either, was from a town called Effingham. I loved them both dearly. One day the subject of mixed-race marriages came up. Sharon and I asked Stan if he would consider dating or even marrying someone who was Black. He emphatically replied, "No way! There is no way I could ever do that," he said.

I was crushed by the response. I did wonder if in the interim, he had forgotten that I was Black. It didn't change my feelings about my dear friend, but it did make me wonder why he couldn't understand, especially if he cared about me the way he said he did, how the response would affect me.

In a way I felt like his response insinuated that Black people were somehow less than, and that he saw himself as being a cut above. It was extremely hurtful. The conversation came up a few more times after that and brought the same response from him, which was never any less painful.

Don't get me wrong. People should be able to have preferences and make choices because of those preferences. I am attracted to men who are a lot taller than I am. If you ask me about dating a man who is shorter than I am, I might react in the same way Stan did that day. I would not, however, react that way if I'm in a room with a guy who is two or three inches shorter than I am.

It boils down to assessing your audience before making a statement. As I write about it now, I wish I could have questioned Stan more and delved a bit more into his feelings about the issue.

Could we chalk the whole scenario up to preferences? That's another book because the answer to that question is absolutely not. Think about it: I didn't grow up being told that short people were inferior or that I had privilege because I was tall or even that if I were tall, that would make me a cut above short people.

It is my opinion that my dear friend Stan had been brought up to believe that Black people were inferior, and even though he opened up and allowed a friendship with me, he came to the table with a plethora of prejudices and biases that had been passed on to him by his family and/or ancestors.

I am happy we became friends because his friendship with me was admittedly the only one he had ever had with an African American before meeting me. I hope our relationship, which meant the world to me, was the beginning of his future quest to further bridge the gap between himself and those around him who are different.

The Gym.

While at a local gym, on another occasion, I was running on the treadmill. There were five other people on various machines around me. As I recall, there were two people exercising on the row of treadmills that I was on and three people behind me on the Stairmaster.

The gym employee entered the room carrying a stack of hand towels. She walked up to the people on the Stairmaster machines and offered them towels and then walked over to the treadmills. There was a person on my left and a person on my right. I was on the treadmill between the two people.

By the time the woman handed out the third towel, I was thinking, "What a pleasure to have joined this gym. This special touch that I am about to experience is the kind of thing that puts this business above the rest."

By the time the gym employee reached the treadmills, I found myself smiling through my sweat. I'm thinking to myself, "Wow, this is great!" I was on my second mile and I was soaked. I figured she would notice that and offer me a towel first, especially since the other clients on the treadmills were walking and not sweating at all.

The woman with the towels walked past me and handed a towel to the guy on my left. There I was, drenched in sweat; I mean the sweat was pouring; it was dripping off my face, onto the floor of the treadmill and all over the rest of the machine.

Sweat was even flying over to the machine next to me and I promise I am not exaggerating. I can see and hear my youngest son cringing and saying, "Ugh, Mom, TMI, (which means "too much information.") He's obviously seen me in this condition before when I was exercising and would cringe at the sight of it.

The woman with the towels then walks to the woman on my right. "Unbelievable! Am I invisible? What the heck? Is it me or did she just walk past me?" There are five white people in the room with towels to wipe their sweat (if they ever break a sweat), and I'm sweating like there's no tomorrow and I have nothing.

Anyone who knows me well can tell you that I absolutely hate to interrupt my workout. But I am hurt, humiliated and not the only one who has noticed the infraction. My exercise comrade gave me that eye contact that almost said, "I don't believe it either."

I slow my pace, eventually stopping the treadmill and getting off. I grab a paper towel and dry off a little. The last thing I want to do is approach this woman looking like the angry sweaty Black woman. When I have her attention I politely say, "Excuse me, I noticed that you offered everyone a towel that was exercising near me and you didn't offer me one."

She said, just as politely, "Oh, I'm sorry, I didn't see you." Right now, I know my critics are probably saying, "Give the woman a break. It could be possible that she didn't see you."

Okay, it's your prerogative to label these incidences any way you want to. My goal is to hopefully raise awareness about our behavior toward others. Call it whatever you want. The next time you're handing out towels at the local gym, give one to every person in the room because the…, "I didn't see you," statement directed at the only person in the room who looks different; the one who is exercising so feverishly that the machine is as loud as ever, is ludicrous at best.

Sell that response to someone who doesn't know any better, or as my grandmother used to say, to someone who was born yesterday. I've been on the planet for more than half a century.

The Costume Store

I rented costumes from a store in my community for a variety show performance at the local television station that a friend and I were producing. The reason for my initial visit to the store was to first find out if the owner had the costumes I needed and see if I could get a good price on the rental. I needed costumes for the three main characters in the popular children's show, The Wizard of Oz: One of my favorite shows of all times by the way.

The owner searched until she found what I needed, allowed me to do a once over, and said she would have them cleaned and ready when I returned. I gave her a deposit for the items, and she told me I would need to pay the balance on the rental when I picked up the costumes.

My visit to the store had been very pleasant. The owner's customer service was phenomenal. Furthermore, I had succeeded in finding exactly what I needed, and she had succeeded in making a few extra bucks: A win win situation. I love it when a plan comes together.

I returned to the store a week later to pick up the rented items. When I walked inside, I had to walk a few feet in a straight line to get to the owner who was standing at the cash register. A middle-aged white man was standing next to her. While walking toward them, I noticed that he went into what seemed to me to be a bit of a panic.

"Close the register!" he said strongly but quietly. The woman seemed to be confused and in the midst of her confusion, the man said the same words two more times, each time being more emphatic than the last time. "Close it! Close it!" By the time I reached them she had acquiesced, and the register was closed.

It was clear to me that this man, who had never seen me before, thought I was coming into the store to rob the place. The woman, on the other hand, seemed baffled by the man's behavior. I was terribly offended. As I was going through the motions of reminding her of all the things I had returned for, I wondered how I would bring up my feelings about the incident to her.

I was feeling rotten as a result of the man's behavior. I thought about just telling her to refund my deposit and leave without mentioning the incident at all. I instead decided that it would be best for me and for her future customers of color if I brought up the incident with kindness and sincerity. It was important to me to let her know exactly how the incident made me feel.

I started out with my famous, "Excuse me, but do you mind if I ask you a question?" She looked up from what she was doing and gave me her undivided attention. "When I walked into the store, the guy that was standing next to you at the register acted as if he thought I wanted to rob the place or that I would somehow take the money if the register wasn't closed before I reached you," I said.

"Oh no," she said. "That's my delivery person. He was embarrassed because he wasn't dressed appropriately enough to be on the floor when customers were coming into the store. It didn't have anything to do with you at all."

I'm thinking, "Wow—that was good!" How did she think of that so fast? Had she been formulating that response for the whole time since the incident occurred at the register? Did she have a feeling that I might say something, so she got prepared ahead of time? Her response did not make any sense.

Still, I had to give her brownie points for being prepared in the nick of time, with a response. Even though it seemed to be a response that came out of nowhere, a response that kind of left you turning your head from side to side like a puppy responding to a low screeching sound.

Nevertheless, she seemed very prepared and pretty much self-assured when she gave her response. My response to her was, "You know, having people work for you that are uncomfortable with people of color could be bad for your business.

"Oh no, no, no," she said. "It wasn't that at all. He was just embarrassed about what he was wearing." She was so convincing (during the second explanation), I could only be glad that she wasn't testifying against me in a jury trial because I would have been in big trouble.

The Perfume Store

I remember one day going into what I'll call a popular perfume store. Three women, who happened to be white, walked in ahead of me. One woman walked in alone and two of the women walked into the store side by side. The salesperson turned twice toward the door each time the women made their entrance and exchanged a cheerful good morning.

I am not extremely far behind the last two women who walked in and both doors are wide open, so it was easy for me to observe the pleasant exchange taking place between the woman behind the register and the women walking into the store.

I was thinking to myself, "I'm going to enjoy being in this store; what a pleasant environment. It's becoming more and more seldom that you find places with great customer service." I was so impressed and encouraged seeing these kinds of pleasantries at a time where people seem to want to take more and give less.

I walked in behind the pair of white women and I looked toward the same cashier to greet her with an expression of gratitude. She didn't look my way. All the cheerfulness had disappeared into whatever she was doing at the counter because it seemed to immediately consume her attention when I walked through the door.

I walked over to the counter and politely said, "Excuse me, but I noticed that you spoke to the three women that walked in before me, but you did not speak to me when I came in." She looked up from whatever it was that had consumed her attention when I walked in the door and said, "Oh, I'm sorry. I didn't see you."

I'm not holding you to anything as a reader. You still have the option of deciding whether an encounter is racially motivated or not. I'm sure that there is probably someone reading this right now who is saying to themselves, "That didn't seem racist to me. Black people are just too sensitive."

I admit to being sensitive, but not too sensitive. The name of this chapter is "Racism Hurts," and I could fill another book with the number of times I have been hurt by it. I pointed out a few experiences because I would like to see Americans politely point out racist behavior on a more regular basis.

You still have every right to label this experience as you see it. As a writer, I guarantee you I don't want to do anything to tick you off to the point where you will stop reading. Further, if I decide to author another book, I'll want you to read that one too.

Let me say this... I didn't understand rappers or hip-hop artists either until I really started to listen to them. I am still filled with gratitude over the education I got from the movie, "Straight Outta Compton" a 2015 film that was produced by Ice Cube and others, directed by F. Gary Gray and written by S. Leigh Savidge, Alan Wenkus and Andrea Berloff.

After being Black and on this planet for more than a half century, I have had the unwelcome opportunity to be hurt by racism on a regular basis, I have gotten the education. For me, it's as clear as the nose on my face and once again I want to thank Keith Olbermann for pointing it out years ago at every turn. I wouldn't be at all surprised if he had to pay a price for it.

My response to the woman behind the counter was, "Well, how are you this morning?" "Oh, I'm fine. Thank you," was her response. Sometimes there is nothing more you can do besides exercise forgiveness and that is exactly what I did that day.

I mentioned earlier that my ex-husband grew up in Bremen, Indiana, in an all-white farming community. The first time I visited Bremen with him, the whole town got wind that I was coming and when we drove through the downtown area, people were standing on the street as if they were waiting for a parade. It was big news, but not quite the kind that they were happy about. And even though they weren't thrilled, because the town's people had a strong Christian background, they behaved accordingly.

As I mentioned earlier, my ex-husband admitted getting negative press about African Americans from the media, his peers and his family and friends. Although he learned later that the information was inaccurate, it left him feeling leery about interacting with people of color.

This brings me back around to my belief that exposure, education and experience are a big part of the process that will move us away from stereotyping, pre-judging and ultimately engaging in racist behavior. Believe it or not, if you're questioning whether or not you have racist behavior and further don't want to hurt anyone, you can take the Implicit Association Test by Harvard University where you determine if you are a racist.

I took the test myself and realized there are some things I need to work on, like learning more about other cultures and religions. We can all begin work on specific issues: we can make friends with people from other cultures that do more than come to our house to get married (because we're a Justice of the Peace) or use our bathroom while they're there. Unfortunately, I am not making this stuff up and it just keeps coming.

When We're Mistaken About Bias

I was recently visiting with a friend in Boca Raton, Florida. One early morning on a fitness center rendezvous, I encountered an unfamiliar security guard who made me literally feel like I was signing my life away in order to use the remote control for the television in the exercise room.

I filled out all the necessary paperwork, which I hadn't had to do on mornings before, and went on my way. About 20 minutes later he came into the center to tell me that he would be changing shifts and that I should give the remote to the a.m. shift security personnel. I slowed down the treadmill, turned down the television and reassured him that I would give the TV remote to the a.m. security guard on duty.

Twenty-five minutes later, he returned and said, since I had been exercising for 45 minutes, I would need to return the remote to him before he ended his shift. This time I turned the volume on the television all the way down because now I'm thinking it's time for me to give this guy a piece of my mind. I said, "I will return the remote when I am finished using it." He responded by saying, "What is your last name again?"

I responded by saying, "I don't think I gave you my last name," knowing full well that before I got that remote, I had given him my full name and added my rank and serial number. He abruptly walked out of the room.

Lots of things ran through my mind after he left and two of the nicest things were, "Does he think I need to steal a remote control?" and "I'm so offended!" I returned the remote control to the a.m. security guard and almost expected to get a slap on the hand for not returning it to the guy on the overnight shift.

The following morning, I walked up to the same "keeper of the remote," and asked if I could use it in the fitness center. After filling out the necessary document, I said to him, "You know—I just have to tell you. I was offended after you gave me the third "remote" reminder yesterday. He asked me why I felt that way. I said, "Because I felt like you were treating me like I was going to steal the remote control. I didn't tell him that I also thought he was treating me that way because I was Black.

To my surprise, he said, "I never thought you were going to steal the remote. I was just making sure that I was doing my job. I don't really see too many people this early in the morning and I hadn't seen you before, so I didn't know for sure if you knew the rules."

"Oh," I said, starting to feel a little better about the situation. He went on to say that he was 82 years old and felt his good health at 82 was result of his lifelong exercise regime. "I used to exercise just like you," he said.

His sharing about his past exercise habits made me feel a connection. We went on to talk about the benefits of taking care of your health by eating right and getting the right amount of exercise.

He even went a few steps farther to talk to me about his feelings toward his own death. He shared that he did not want to suffer and that he hoped he would either die in his sleep or have a massive heart attack. "I concur," I told him with a laugh in my voice.

He asked if he could call upstairs to my friend's condo if he ever started feeling bad and needed to talk to someone for reassurance, (I assumed he may have had a medical condition because of his request). I told him I had a couple of days left to visit but if something happened before I left, I would be happy to come down and sit with or talk to him.

I walked away and as a result of our conversation, I felt a connection. No one could have told me that I would connect with this guy on this level. I felt that I had done the very thing that I accuse others of doing, jumping to conclusions without knowing the whole story. I also felt a little sad for my new friend who at 82, still had to endure working on a graveyard or overnight shift. Even though I am a few decades younger, I thought about how difficult it would be for me to stay awake all night and keep a 30-unit building secure.

The moral of this story is we all must stop judging books by their cover and making assumptions. We need to focus more on how we treat people rather than on how people are treating us.

In his book, The Four Agreements, Don Miguel Ruiz states, "The way to keep yourself from making assumptions is to ask questions. Make sure the communication is clear. If you don't understand, ask. Have the courage to ask questions until you are clear as you can be, and even then, do not assume you know all there is to know about a given situation. Once you hear the answer, you will not have to make assumptions because you will know the truth."

This story about my security guard friend is a good example of an assumption gone wrong. I agree with Ruiz in that if we start talking to people more and stop making assumptions, the world would be a better place.

I would like to add that we also need to take a few extra minutes to do a better job of understanding things we misunderstand. We are all unique, wonderfully made, talented and flawed. We should all take time to ask questions, and either be prepared for the answer we were not expecting or be prepared to connect with someone on a heart-to-heart level.

How easy is it for us to be indifferent towards things that we don't understand? Even the smallest nuances can be misinterpreted. Once while taking an evening break at work I decided to get healthier faire for lunch from the local grocery store across the street from my workplace.

While standing in line at the register I became annoyed by a woman who was standing very close to me. She was so far into my personal space that I had to keep inching away from her. For me, it was extremely uncomfortable.

I was relieved when I was able to finish my purchase and get out of line and away from the woman. I did notice before I left the store that the woman who had been in my space and standing so close, appeared to be Chinese.

When I returned to work, I sought out my Chinese co-worker and asked her if she could educate me, or just let me know if there was a cultural reason (that I didn't understand) why the woman in the store was standing in such close proxemics.

My co-worker told me that it was quite possible that the woman had recently moved to the United States and was not yet accustomed to dealing with Americans and their personal space. She explained to me, through a little humorous role-playing, that China is very crowded and that its inhabitants are accustomed to being in close proxemics with one another.

"In some cases, she explained, "People are physically touching while moving about from one place to another." After receiving the information, I was glad that I hadn't been rude to the woman. Annoyed, yes, but rude, no. I was grateful to have a coworker and friend who was open to educating me about her culture despite my ignorance.

Or at least I thought that was the case, until my friend started behaving with indifference toward me. I believe, even though she denies it, that she was offended by my ignorance regarding her culture. Even though I learned something, I lost a friendship.

The place where I go to get my nails done is owned by a Vietnamese family. For years I noticed that when the family members communicated with one another, they would rarely, if ever, look in the direction of the person they were talking to. Eventually, I became curious enough to ask why one sister never made eye contact when she was having a conversation with someone.

For Americans, most of us find it rude not to make eye contact with the people we are talking to or interacting with. They explained to me that in Vietnamese culture, it is rude to make eye contact when having a conversation with another person.

While training to become a Court Appointed Special Advocate for Abused and Neglected Children (CASA), I took part in a training seminar that was led by a probation officer. The session focused on racial tolerance and cultural differences. The training was an attempt to help us as volunteers to be open to the cultural differences of the children and families we would be serving. It left me feeling educated and enlightened. I even learned something about myself.

The trainer cautioned us about judging youth because of the way they related in terms of communication. For example, she told us that for most Americans, we tend to judge a person critically when they cannot make eye contact with the receiver when communicating. Many times, we decide that perhaps the person cannot be trusted or that they're trying to hide something. When a person cannot make eye contact, it even raises our suspicions about that person.

The trainer went on to explain that there are other reasons a person is unable to make eye contact when communicating one-on-one. The information she shared immediately hit home for me. She explained that sometimes in the African American community a child could be reprimanded for looking an adult directly in the eye when the adult is speaking to them.

In other words, indirect eye contact could be related to upbringing, especially in the Black community. Personally, I can look a person directly in the eye whenever I am addressing them. However, when they address me, my eyes immediately begin to drop or move around the room.

Until the training, I had not given it much thought because no one had ever brought it to my attention. But because of the training, I realized that growing up in the house with my grandmother exposed me to statements such as this: "Don't you dare look at me that way when I'm talking to you." "If you look at me like that again, you'll be sorry."

Because of my grandmother's threats and because I didn't know how I was looking at her, my gaze would eventually start to drop whenever I spoke to her. I noticed later that in one-on-one conversations with others, I struggled to maintain eye contact. Forty years later, I still have to force myself to look a person in the eye when they are talking to me.

If I had to guess, I would say that this whole situation originated with slavery. It is my feeling that the slave/master relationship was one where many times the slave was required to drop their gaze when being spoken to. A close friend of mine told me recently that when he was fifteen years old and living in Mississippi, (post slavery) he looked into the eyes of his white employer and the man slapped his face.

According to my friend, the man followed up with the words, "Don't you ever look at me that way again!" In some weird sort of way, slavery perpetuated this behavior and then passed it from generation to generation.

There are other issues as well, because of slavery, that continue to stigmatize the Black community in modern-day life. We cannot seem to get over this feeling that we're spoiling our infants. One definition I encountered said to spoil is to make useless or to damage; to let a person have his or her own way so much that they demand or expect it. In my experience, growing up in the Black community, this concept is often attached to very young children.

When a child is picked up because they're crying, we risk spoiling them. If we rock, cuddle or hold them after all their needs have been met (meaning they're dry, fed and healthy) we're spoiling them, damaging them and making them useless.

I know that some of you are aghast at the accusation. Let me be clear. No one behavior applies to an entire group of people. I cuddled and spoiled my children to the chagrin of a lot of my peers. If I wanted to hold them while they slept, I felt like it was my prerogative.

Some of the babies I cared for had to adjust to the attention they received because a couple of little ones that I fostered had been left in a crib for extended periods without receiving any cuddling at all. Apparently, they were in the care of someone who believed that spoiling could be detrimental.

They were indifferent about being touched initially but soon grew to love it. I remember a close friend warning me about giving them more affection than I gave my own kids. They needed it and I remain unapologetic. Yes, I do think that the idea of infant-spoiling dates all the way back to slavery.

The Criminal's
Life Matters

Convincing the world at large that the criminal or the person who is justice involved has a life that matters is a hard sell. But I am a firm believer that *hurt* people *hurt* people. The author of "The Five Love Languages of God," Gary Chapman, talks about how full and empty love tanks can affect a young person's psyche: "Much of the violence among teenagers in our society is rooted in their having empty love tanks," says Chapman.

"In the heart of the teenager, love has to do with connection, acceptance and nurturing," Chapman continued. He believes we should all have at least five people in our lives whose eyes light up when we walk into a room. This is just one of the gifts that help to fill our love tanks.

As a society, we do a lot of engaging in the lives of people after they become criminals. The world will only begin to heal when we begin to focus on the juvenile along with their family. The earlier this happens, the better.

While we regularly complain about the rising number of offenders entering the penitentiary or about the heinousness of their crimes, we would rather picket outside of an abortion clinic than mentor an unwanted child who is already here.

I've said it before, and I'll say it again. In order to dial down the number of people in our criminal justice system, we have to combat child abuse. I hear it all the time, "It starts at home," or What are the parents doing?" or "Parents are not paying attention to their kids." Or fill in the blank.

These statements make sense when there are parents available for the kids; as long as Mom is not dealing with an alcohol, heroin or crack addiction; it makes sense when kids are not having to fend for themselves; it makes sense when Mom or Dad don't have a mental illness and kids are in a household filled with abuse and dysfunction.

Dysfunction is powerful and it takes a significant amount of work to combat it. As a court appointed special advocate for abused and neglected children (CASA), I have had an opportunity to work with mothers whose children were in foster care. For example, I worked with a mother who had two kids who had been taken away from her due to neglect.

As the CASA on a DCFS case, I visited the mother, the children, the foster parents, the schools the children attended, communicated with the guardian ad litem (GAL) or the attorney who looks out for the best interest of the child. I also communicated with the Mom's attorney. All of this was an effort to reunify the family. It was a long process with an outcome that was always unpredictable. A young child is known to be able to break through the chains of dysfunction if intervention is started early.

The Head Start Program, sponsored by the United States Department of Human Services, and the first publicly funded preschool program, was created in 1965 by President Johnson. The federal government helped create this half-day program for preschool children from low-income families. Head Start began as a summer pilot program that included an education component, nutrition and health screenings for children, and support services for families.

In the 1960's only ten percent of the nation's three and four-year-old children were enrolled in a classroom setting. By 2005, sixty-nine percent of four-year-old children nationwide participated in some type of state preschool program. (www.k12academics.com)

Head Start is a good starting place for at-risk children. More programs like this one, with initiatives geared toward support for the adolescent can contribute to a marked decrease in the number of individuals who become residents in our penal system.

"In 2019 the Head Start community welcomed a significant increase in federal funding." (www.nhsa.org)

"After months of stalemate and shutdowns in Congress, the Head Start community welcomes this significant increase in funding for a foundational American program that gives nearly one million of our most vulnerable children a head start in life every year." National Head Start Association, NSHA, Executive Director, Yasmina Vinci said.

According to the National Priorities Project, "Being poor takes a real toll on kids, but those who attend a quality preschool are more likely to graduate from high school, earn more as adults, and are less likely to become teen parents, serve jail or prison time, [etc]."

In the book, Guilt by Reason of Insanity: A Psychiatrist Probes the Minds of Killers. Dorothy Otnow Lewis, MD, interviews clients who are killers and have sustained significant abuse in their childhood experiences.

In a New York Times article entitled, "Damaged Brains and the Death Penalty, Laura Mansnerus interviewed Dr. Lewis along with longtime collaborator, Dr. Jonathan H. Pincus, the chief of neurology at the Veterans Administration Hospital in Washington.

In a study done by the two doctors, "Of the fourteen juveniles sentenced to death, the researchers found that all had suffered head trauma, most in car accidents but many by beatings as well. Twelve had suffered brutal physical abuse, five of those sodomized by relatives.

"No one suggests that abuse or brain damage makes a person a murderer, but Dr. Lewis says that while most damaged people do not turn into killers, almost every killer is a damaged person."

She concludes that most murderers are shaped by the combination of damage to the brain, particularly to the frontal lobes. The frontal lobes control aggression and impulsiveness. But more complex damage is caused by repeated, violent child abuse.

We are affected by what we bring to the table. Our experiences as children shape who we become as adults. As a parent who fostered teens, I have lived with young people who have spent time in the juvenile detention center. Some of the same kids grew up and spent time in adult correctional facilities. These are individuals that I cared deeply for.

Some of the kids came to me with empty love tanks. Some of them had survived emotional, physical and sexual abuse in their homes. Some of these atrocities occurred in the homes of foster parents who were ill equipped to deal with the damage some of these children had experienced.

There is an ongoing belief that there are more Black men in prison than any other race in our nation. The fact is you would be surprised by the statistics regarding African American men in our penal system in the United States. In 2013, in a poll taken by the American Council on Education, "there were 1,437,363 Black men in college and 745,000 incarcerated.

But some in that smaller number of young Black men can find themselves detained as a result of gang activity. According to Jimmy Dee, not his real name, a former member of a well-known gang, the problem for most young Black men is the absence of the father figure in the home. Dee said he believes this leaves the door wide open for the gang member to approach the youth and recruit them to into the gang's family.

"When I was released from prison, the gang was there to bless me; they provided me with money, liquor, drugs, women; all the things they thought would make me happy were included in their blessing, he said.

The gang becomes the father the young person did not have; the close friend and confidante. According to Dee, they were there when there is no one else around. Now if as a society, we could somehow provide a similar support system, these young men might be less apt to find themselves joining gangs.

"At the Pendleton Juvenile Detention Center, to curtail gang violence, the Center has devised a therapeutic program that brings rival gangs together. For example, you would have Vice Lords and the Gangster Disciples on the same turf, so to speak.

Under different circumstances, when either of the gangs make contact with an individual from a rival gang, they are taught to beat one another down. But under these circumstances, they're left with no other choice besides leveling the playing field. According to Pendleton officials, the young men can even be seen embracing one another.

British actor Tim Roth, a Deception Expert and Social Scientist who was on the Fox television show, "Lie to Me," made this statement on one of his episodes: "Do you know how to create a disturbed personality? You do it with constant criticism and lack of affection."

This statement describes the ingredients for a difficult road to rehabilitation during incarceration. As one ex-offender put it, "In prison, there's nothing positive. You don't get rehabilitated there; what you learn [is] how to become a better criminal."

Yes, people in prison commit crimes and sometimes, those crimes are unimaginable; but prison is like society in that there are all kinds of people in prison, including some who are innocent and some, as strange as it may seem, who rehabilitate.

Further, if we are allowing people in prison to be raped, shanked, killed, etc., what does that say about us? By allowing these things to happen, in my opinion, we are exhibiting criminal behavior ourselves.

What is wrong when an inmate has to become a vigilante in prison in an effort to protect weaker prisoners? In an article written by Nick Chester, entitled, "Meet the Vigilante Prisoner Who Beats Up Jail Rapists." The article states that T-Bone is a 6'5" ex-marine who believes it is his Christian duty to protect weaker inmates from being sexually abused.

The article goes on to say that T-Bone himself has been stabbed and beat to within inches of his life as a result. Really! Who is in charge at this prison and why aren't we bringing criminal charges against this act of aiding and abetting?

I know that for some, people in prison have become those who are out of sight and out of mind. I am encouraged by the fact that there are so many television programs that shed light on prisons around the United States. I hope that this will begin to make a difference in what happens behind prison walls.

I've heard people in the general public say, "Inmates have it good: They get three meals a day, some of them are allowed to have televisions, they get to buff up (exercise), etc.

Let me just say this: As a criminal social justice professional who has worked with men who are released from Cook County Jail, volunteered with women and juveniles who were detained in Cook and DuPage County, there is nothing good about jail or prison. Just being there is enough.

People should not have to fear for their lives 24 hours a day. And people certainly should not have to spend time in solitary confinement for an exorbitant amount of time. What good comes from this?

While I'm talking about solitary confinement, I feel like I need to mention one other thing that has been under my skin for years. Jeff Fort, co-founder of the Black P. Stone Nation has been in prison in Florence, Colorado under a no-human-contact order since 2006.

Where is the humanity? After 40 years in prison and after reaching the age of 73, ADX Florence prison personnel cannot contain a 73-year-old unless he has no human contact. Let my record reflect that I stand in opposition of solitary confinement and in opposition to no-human-contact orders over an unreasonable amount of time.

I have a question: Who are we? In our arrogance, we turn our noses up at the criminal. We spend time talking about how vicious and cruel the crimes are that they commit, and then we turn around, like someone has given us a license, and we are as vicious and cruel as the offender. I have two words: STOP IT!

I know someone is probably saying that I'm so concerned for the perpetrator that I must not care about the victim. I care enough to have pursued higher education in criminal justice so that I can be a part of the solution for the victim as well as the perpetrator.

I've said it before, and I'll say it again. I believe one of the only ways to curtail crime is to eradicate child abuse. You can look at me and say, "That's ridiculous. But there are a lot of people in prison and in juvenile detention who are the products of unspeakable abuse. How do I know? I was a foster parent; I volunteered in juvenile detention; I was a Court Appointed Special Advocate for Abused and Neglected Children (CASA); I have worked with adult men who are justice involved who shared their stories of abuse with me.

Hurt people hurt people. According to the Bureau of Justice Statistics, sixty percent of released prisoners become repeat offenders. These statistics alone should be reason enough to search for more alternative rehabilitation options for offenders because their lives do matter.

The POTUS'
Life Matters

"President Obama has endured the vilest sort of disrespect that we and the world have ever seen, and we as a nation are lessened by it. It's an embarrassment and an eye opener because it has become evident that prejudice and bigotry are alive and well within our country. Through it all, our President has carried himself in an outstanding manner and has shown what the embodiment of class looks like. Shame on those that bring shame on us all." (fb/-Jerry Myers, Occupy Democrats member)

I was having a conversation with a very good friend about an experience I had in the workplace while providing part-time care for seniors in their homes. I was on an assignment with a 97-year-old who had an around-the-clock caregiver. I was there to fill in on an overnight shift so the regular daytime caregiver could rest at night.

I was expected to sit in a room that was used as a den and located directly outside the client's room. The woman's daughter, who planned to stay in the home for the first few nights I was there, asked if I could leave the television and my computer off because she believed it would disturb her mother.

She also told me that having a light on would disturb her mother as well. I told her I might find it difficult to sit in the dark for a 12-hour shift, so she turned on a low light in the bathroom that was located next to the den.

While relaying the experience to my friend, she asked if I thought the daughter's behavior had anything to do with racism. I told her I wasn't sure if her behavior was related to racism or some kind of superiority syndrome. I did feel like it was important to her that I be continually reminded that I was only "the help."

Unfortunately, this racist tone is apparent all over America. I believe people were so incensed by Obama's election that things got more out of hand. It has been noted that after Obama took office, the number of white supremacy groups in the United States increased. What this says to me is even though it took 200 years to elect an African American to the office of the President, there are still a lot of people who are not happy about it.

Earlier I mentioned that I worked for a company that had almost 15,000 people working in their warehouse and there was only one African American manager. For those of you who don't know where I'm going with this, let me paint a picture.

When I work for you and you have ten managers on staff and not one of them is African American, you're making a very clear statement to me. And what I'd like to express to you is this: We can't be what we can't see. But if you don't care about me, you wouldn't care about that either.

Further, when it takes more than 200 years for us to put an African American in the White House, that is just one more way you're confirming that Black people don't measure up. So once there is someone in the White House who looks like me, or looks like my father or my brother, I resist any negative opinion that you have about him.

A few years ago, I reconnected with a very close friend through Facebook. She lives in a suburban town near Atlanta. During a weeklong visit with her, I logged in a countless number of hours at the apartment gym while my friend was working. On one occasion I met a very friendly fellow who took extra time to communicate with me even though he was finishing his workout when I arrived at the gym.

He was white, about 24 years old, which I assumed because he mentioned he had graduated from high school six years earlier. He said he was married and had two young children ages six and four.

We had a great time sharing about many different subjects. I learned he was a musician and composer. However, he said he felt as if it were time for him to stop chasing his dream and grow up. He shared that he had decided to join the Navy and would do his initial training at Great Lakes in Illinois.

Somewhere in between talking about North Korea, South Korea and war in general, he brought up "my" president. "I don't know about Barack Obama," he said. "I think he's too much of an idealist." My first thought was, "Here we go."

Let me say this: It was not the worst thing you could say about a person. I could even be construed as a nice thing, but the subject of Obama is not conversational territory you want to venture into with me especially if you're not on my side... and the same goes for Oprah Winfrey.

Furthermore, on some level, it makes me feel a little apprehensive about your motives when you're questioning me about another African American. I believe this comes from years of people waiting until I'm in a room full of white people and deciding to ask me things like... "so Kelley, what do you think of Muhammed Ali or Shirley Chisholm or Maya Angelou, etc. Their response after I answered would usually be negative press about the person.

David Horowitz is the founder of the David Horowitz Freedom Center, a think tank in Los Angeles created to combat "the efforts of the radical left and it's Islamist allies to destroy American values." Regarding Barack Obama and what he believes to be Black privilege, Horowitz said, "Black privilege also extends to the White House. Barack Obama was an inexperienced presidential candidate who was elected because Americans wanted to experience a post-racial sugar high," says Horowitz.

Colin Powell has, what I believe, is a very nice counter (even though he is responding to another person):

"Let me just be candid: my party is full of racists, and the real reason a considerable portion of my party wants President Obama out of the White House has nothing to do with the content of his character, nothing to do with his competence as Commander-in-Chief and President, and everything to do with the color of his skin, and that's despicable." (Colin Powell, (R), Huffington Post)

Did I want Obama to succeed at becoming the first African American President of the United States because he was Black? I would be lying if I didn't admit that that was one of the reasons. However, there are so many other reasons. President Obama is competent, charismatic, intelligent, educated, a great family man, a one-in-a-million public speaking phenomenon, a world changer, an encourager and a bit of a quiet storm. We never get too old for role models, and Obama is definitely one of mine.

Since Obama took office, he has been such an encouragement to me. And he continues to encourage me and the rest of the world outside of the office of the President. He just genuinely cares so much for his community and the world. He recently shared this tribute to the late Aretha Franklin on Facebook:

"America has no royalty. But we do have a chance to earn something enduring. Born in Memphis and raised in Detroit, Aretha Franklin grew up performing gospel songs in her father's congregation. For more than six decades since, every time she sang, we were all graced with the glimpse of the divine.

Through her compositions and unmatched musicianship, Aretha helped define the American experience. In her voice, we could feel our history, all of it and in every shade—our power and our pain, our darkness and our light, our quest for redemption and our hard-won respect. She helped us feel more connected to each other, more hopeful, more human. And sometimes she helped us forget about everything else and dance."

"Aretha may have passed on to a better place, but the gift of her music remains to inspire us all. May the Queen of Soul rest in eternal peace. Michelle and I send our prayers and warmest sympathies to her family and all those moved by her song." - *President Barack Obama*

I love this tribute and I love the response to this tribute written in a Facebook post by Darlene Parker.

"This is how a President speaks. Thank you, Mr. President. You will always and forever be the president I see as our country's finest. We will have another chance once we walk out of this darkness we are in currently. I hope one day again in my lifetime,

our country knows a president with your intelligence, grace, integrity and spirit."

My sentiment exactly!

Yes, Obama is in fact, one of my favorite role models. He has encouraged me to be "a part of the change" I want to see in the world. He has inspired me. He has given me figurative wings to fly. In the words of the popular song by Bette Midler, he has become, "the wind beneath my wings."

President Obama has inspired me to become a better me and to reach higher goals. Since Obama's election, I have completed a master's program and have been inspired to finish my first book. The book that you are holding in your hands or reading and/or listening to on your tablet of phone right now.

"I know your works. See, I have set before you an open door, and no one can shut it..." (Revelation 3:8)

I've said it before, and I believe it. There are three ways to combat racism, prejudice and bias, and it is through experience, education and exposure. We must also deal with it in a spirit of intelligence and excellence.

My former president is the ultimate role model for confronting everything with intelligence and excellence! He is a model of integrity that, in the face of the rest of the world, makes a lot of us want to be just like him.

The way he handles racism is a lesson to us all: I've never heard him say it, but I can imagine him giving this kind of advice in the face of it; I can even hear him directing advice toward himself sounding something like this: "You just need to pick yourself up, dust yourself off and keep it moving." Or he simply hears his First Lady and ours,

Michelle Obama's famous words which are: "When they go low, we go high."

I remember my mother reading the poem, "Mother to Son," to me by Langston Hughes, a man who decried racism and injustice. It became a form of great encouragement to me. While reading the words recently I thought of our former president and some to the figurative stairs he had to climb while in office. If only we really knew, right?

Mother to Son, by Langston Hughes

Well son, I'll tell you:
Life for me ain't been no crystal stair.
It had tacks in it,
And splinters,
And boards torn up,
And places with no carpet on the floor-
Bare.
But all the time
I'se been-a-climbin' on
And reaching landings,
And turnin' corners,
And sometimes goin' in the dark
Where there ain't no light.
So [chile], don't you turn back.
Don't you sit down on the steps
'Cause you find it's kinder hard.
Don't you fall now-
For I'se still goin' honey
I'se still climbin',
And life for me ain't been no crystal stair.

The good news is that President Obama came through it with dignity and finesse always and in all ways and by doing so he has been an encouragement to so many. No matter what happened, he kept giving to the American people in big and small ways.

As a part-time caregiver, I once worked in the home of an attorney who knew the Obamas. I noticed right away that he was in several framed photos with President Obama at the White House. He also had a signed letter from the President that was on his mantle as well.

Curiosity hit me like a flash of lightning and of course I had questions. I found out that this attorney had been up close and personal with the Obamas in what he considered to be a friendship. When I asked him how he would describe the President, he said, "I have never seen compassion and intellect come together in anyone the way it has for this man." My heart welled!

It was also an inspiration to see the joy in the face of the 106-year-old who danced as a result of her excitement over meeting the President and First Lady at the White House. We are never too old for role models and President Obama is the cream of the crop.

Remember the company I mentioned earlier. They had roughly 1,500 employees with one African American manager. The "powers that be" assured me that they had a couple of African American managers at their Atlanta office.

I bring this company up again to point out that I can't be what I can't see.

This be-what-I-can't-see story brings me back to that long-awaited day when someone else who looked like me won the election and became the 44th President of the United States of America. My jaws are hurting from smiling as I write this. I smile every time I remember that day. And what a day it was!

After more than 200 years of presidencies and 43 presidential terms, my children (tears) and grandchildren can shoot for the stars, or even the presidency. A Black man had finally won a presidential election.

The point is the result of Obama's election sends a different message through that same bullhorn. And I get to hear it along with a countless number of others: "You do measure up!"

My best friend, who I mentioned earlier, holds a PhD in social work from Loma Linda University in California. She responded to Obama's election by saying, "I hope this will motivate more people in the nation to stop settling for mediocrity in their own lives." For years, this friend had tried talking me into returning to school for a Master's degree. Less than a year after the election, I was back in school.

My best friend has been pushing me to get a PhD since I graduated. I jokingly told her if Obama ran for second term, I might go for it. I lied. The truth is my hat's off to all the PhDs in the world, but I just don't want to work that hard. When it comes to acquiring my master's degree, I am sure that my desire to return to school was causally related to Obama winning the 2008 presidential election. What a motivation!

Despite the glamor of the presidency, I'm sure President Obama faced some tough times while he was in office. Not only did he have to deal with the usual complaints coming from those who disagreed with his policies, he also had to deal with people who felt like he didn't measure up because he was Black.

This is indicative of many things, but especially by the upsetting and disrespectful images of the President and the First Lady that occasionally graced the internet. Not to mention that Congress tried to block almost every good thing Obama tried to do while he was in office.

And what about the smaller issues that came up like Michelle wearing a dress with her arms out, while we have had a first lady who has posed nude; or Obama wearing a brown suit instead of a darker one, when another president thought it was funny to grab women in their private area. The hypocrisy makes me want to holler... but I digress.

Racism is a complex issue. There are more than one or two things that will help us combat it. We need to continue to have open dialog and continue to create new ideas for dealing with the issues that plague not only this country but other countries as well.

Our former president said in one of his speeches, "It is possible to join hands in a common effort." In another quote he said, "We will extend a hand if you're willing to unclench your fist."

We all need to take these quotes literally and not interpret the word "all" with a grain of salt, so to speak. We all have to be willing to extend a hand and we all have to be willing to unclench our fists. As a nation we could make it our new citizen-to-citizen mantra: "Extend a hand, unclench a fist."

This puts me in the mind of the song, "We Shall Overcome," because I think that by extending a hand and unclenching a fist, we will succeed in overcoming the cesspool of intolerance that is plaguing our nation.

I don't believe the presidency has been a "crystal stair" all the time for Obama. I would surmise that it's had thorns in it; boards torn up and places where it seemed there was no carpet on the floor. But I believe our president kept on climbing, turning corners and standing strong, even in very dark places.

Mr. President, you have been such an encouragement to me and to so many others. I would like to, in turn, encourage you with these words from the 26th President of the United States of America, who had some tall challenges of his own as Commander in Chief:

"When you come to the end of your rope, tie a knot and hang on."
-Franklin D. Roosevelt.

President Obama, we have seen you take the high road again and again and again. Thanks for showing us all how to keep on climbin' and how to tie a knot and never let go!

I salute you!

End of Life Matters

After my mother died, and after attending 12-step Co-Dependence Anonymous meetings, I realized two things: I did not know much about death and dying and that I needed to focus on serving people who had no power over the situation they found themselves in.

I bring up my codependence stint because it was a sponsor at Co-Dependence Anonymous (CoDA), who told me more than thirty years ago that if I felt like I just had to serve to feel like a whole person, I needed to volunteer with people who had not created impossible situations for themselves.

"Co-Dependence Anonymous is a twelve-step program for people who share a common desire to develop functional and healthy relationships.

At that time, I chose individuals in hospice. I know when a person gets to the end of their life, there's nothing anyone can do to stop the inevitable, short of a miracle, and nine chances out of ten, it is not their fault that they're dying in the first place.

Even in my codependence, I was at times exhausted supporting those who lacked self-discipline in their lives, who were constantly trying to make their poor planning my emergency. On the other hand, when death comes to call, you have absolutely no control. I knew that this was one of the populations I wanted to volunteer to serve.

I trained to become a hospice volunteer at Northwestern Memorial Hospital on Chicago's near north side. At the time, Northwestern had a ten-bed hospice unit where approximately 30 people died a month; seventy-five percent of the patients on the unit were HIV-positive.

My mother died pre-hospice training and when I was told that she was terminally ill, I could not intellectualize it. I was 30 years old at the time and the news hit me like a ton of bricks. My mother was dying! It couldn't be. There had to be a mistake. I knew that other people died. There was no confusion for me there. But my mother!

I had trouble processing the news. A couple of days before my mother died, she was visiting at my home in Indiana. She called me from Illinois to say she felt a lot sicker than usual. I asked a friend of mine, who lived in the Chicago area, if she would rent a car and drive my mother from Chicago to Indianapolis. She agreed.

I knew my mother was terminal, but I didn't understand anything about death and dying and I was afraid. I became very apprehensive about being with her. What would happen if she died while I was alone in the room with her? What would I do?

Would I immediately die from a broken heart after her death? Would she start gasping for air, start vomiting or worse, start bleeding. The unknowns made me very sad and anxious. My anxiety level on a scale from one to ten was about one hundred – completely off the charts.

Twenty-four hours after arriving at our home in Indianapolis, my mother had to be rushed by ambulance to an unfamiliar hospital in Indianapolis. Her body was ravished with cancer that was causing an enormous amount of pain and discomfort. Since the hospital staff was functioning without medical records, they had to do (what seemed like) every test imaginable.

The entire time my mother was begging me to take her home and make them stop. It's painful reliving the experience. What did the doctors find after all that tortuous testing? They discovered what we knew all the time, that my mother was dying.

The new news was that her bowel had also ruptured; the peritonitis, or poison was distributing itself all over her body. It seemed to be magnifying her pain a hundredfold. She wanted to go home. She said she didn't want to die in a hospital.

For me, handling death at home was probably the most outlandish idea I had ever heard of. I wasn't a doctor. What if there was an emergency? There couldn't be an emergency; my mother was actively dying. If only I'd had all my hospice experience and training before my mother's death. If that had been the case, my mother's transition could have been so much more comfortable and different.

I would have taken her home, and instead of being attached to all the machines that dripped and moaned and presented details about her health, I would have crawled into bed with her and gotten close enough for her to feel my heartbeat as hers faded. I would have stayed that way until she took her last breath.

Now as a trained hospice volunteer, I have come to realize many things; one is that again education, experience and exposure can be life changing and that "end of life" matters. Not only does it matter, but it can be made to be as beautiful and meaningful as the beginning of one's life

I found a poem that kind of sums up society's response to aging. I love to read it because I am moved so much by the sentiment in the words. Legend has it that it is a tale "authored by an anonymous elderly gentleman, living in an Australian nursing home" but there is another story that points to the fact that a female nurse may be responsible.

The bottom line is that elderly people should not be treated as if they're invisible. All of us will either die young or grow old. For those of us who are caring for seniors, we have to remember to respect, honor and treasure their long lives, because their lives matter.

Cranky Old Man

What do you see nurses? What do you see?
What are you thinking…when you're looking at me?
A cranky old man, not very wise, uncertain of habit with faraway
eyes?
Who dribbles his food and makes no reply.
When you say in a loud voice, I do wish you'd try!
Who seems not to notice the things that you do.
And forever is losing a sock or a shoe?
Who, resisting or not, lets you do as you will,
With bathing and feeding, the long day to fill?
Is that what you're thinking? Is that what you see?
I'll tell you who I am as I sit here so still, As
I do your bidding as I eat at your will.
I'm a small child of ten, with a father and mother,
Brothers and sisters who love one another
A young boy of sixteen with wings on his feet
Dreaming that soon now, a lover he'll meet.

A groom son at twenty, my heart gives a leap,
Remembering the vows that I promised to keep.
At twenty-five now, I have young of my own,
Who needs me to guide a secure happy home.
A man of thirty, my young now grown fast.
Bound to each other with ties that should last.
At forty, my young sons are grown and are gone,
But my woman is beside me to see I don't mourn,
At fifty, once more, babies play 'round my knee,'
Again, we know children, my loved ones and me.
Dark days are upon me, my wife is now dead.
I look to the future, I shudder with dread.
For my young are all rearing young of their own,
And I think of the years and the love that I've known.
I'm now an old man and nature is cruel.
It's just to make old age look like a fool.
The body it crumbles, grace and vigor depart.
There is now a stone where I once had a heart.
But inside this old carcass a young man still dwells.
And now and again my battered heart swells.
I remember the joy. I remember the pain.
And I'm loving and living life over again.
I think of the years, all too few, gone too fast.
And accept the stark fact that nothing can last
So open your eyes people, open and see.
Not a cranky old man.
Look closer…see…me!
(Originally by Phyllis McCormack;
Adapted by Dave Griffith)

This poem tells us that we should never diminish the importance of the life of a senior. When we look closer, we will find people who will decorate our lives in ways that no younger individual is capable of doing.

Look closer and see that the senior, no matter what age, is looking for the same things we are at twenty, thirty, forty years or older; the pursuit of happiness. When we "see them" we can become a huge part of making a difference in their lives. The difference that makes them feel like their lives still matter.

As a part-time caregiver for seniors in their homes, I have shared many beautiful experiences with seniors who are healthy and well, and with seniors who were ready to make their transition from life to death. When death is impending, in most cases, hospice is involved.

"Hospice focuses on caring, not curing, and in most cases, care is provided in the patient's home. It is a model for quality, compassionate care for people facing a life limiting illness or injury, hospice care involves a team-oriented approach to expert medical care, pain management, and emotional and spiritual support expressly tailored to the patient's needs and wishes.

Support is provided to the patient's loved ones as well. At the center of hospice and palliative care is the belief that each of us has the right to die pain-free and with dignity, and that our families will receive the necessary support to allow us to do so," (National Hospice and Palliative Care Organization).

As a caregiver, I have had many hospice experiences. All of my experiences have been very different in nature. I would like to share two of the experiences with you. I will change the names of my clients for the purpose of confidentiality.

According to Elisabeth Kubler-Ross in her 1969 book on death and dying, there are five stages that people go through "in response to the knowledge of death." They are commonly referred to an acronym of DABDA, and are denial, anger, bargaining, depression and acceptance." I have often said jokingly that when death comes knocking at my door, I am going out kicking and screaming. One of my clients felt the same way.

I was called to care for someone in hospice who was stuck in the anger stage until the day before she died. She was 87 years old and weighed less than 90 pounds. There was no correlation between her weight and her impending death but later it will become clear why I mentioned it.

She was dying from lung cancer and it had spread to her liver and kidneys, as well as to other parts of her body. Her mobility was compromised because of her declining health. Her medical situation, however, did not stop her from wanting to get out of bed every five minutes to smoke a cigarette; and that's literally every five minutes. It was a bit unusual, but she was an end-of-life heavy smoker. Smoking consumed her days and her thoughts.

The biggest problem with this (aside from the fact that I was mortified by the thought of the second-hand smoke in the room), she also had a huge oxygen tank. She had difficulty holding her cigarette, lighting the cigarette and even taking a drag from the cigarette in order to inhale.

To add insult to injury, because she was so weak at this point, when she attempted to smoke, she went into coughing spasms that took her breath away. After the coughing episodes I would usually end up giving her a breathing treatment and/or hooking her back up to the oxygen tank.

This may all sound a little unreasonable and unrealistic; almost too much to ask of any caregiver, but my client's family believed that their loved one should be able to do whatever she wanted at the end of her life. If that meant she would attempt to smoke a pack of cigarettes a day before she died, then that's just the way it was going to be. This is the reason there were five caregivers before me who refused to stay and take care of her.

I am a person who also believes the end of the fourth quarter of life should bring nothing but joy to the person making their transition. For that reason, I tolerated the cigarette smoking. Furthermore, when you think of all the things a dying person could request, wanting to smoke can become a very small thing.

On the hospice unit at Northwestern, we might have a patient say, "Boy, I wish I had a quarter pounder." As volunteers, if we felt like a request was within our power, we would do our best to grant it. Sometimes after returning and spreading the food out in front of the person, they would say, "I don't want it." They would always be grateful that we went out of our way to fulfill their requests.

The plot did thicken with my client, however. I was on board for getting her in and out of bed to smoke in the daytime but smoking in the middle of the night was a horse of a different color.

Time and time again in the middle of the night I would hear the call: "Help, help, somebody help me!" The first few times I rushed to her bedside for fear she might be experiencing some additional distress, and she would say, "I want to smoke a cigarette."

"It's the middle of the night Marjorie; you'll have to wait until tomorrow," I would tell her. When I would walk away, she would continue screaming "help" until I acquiesced. After watching her doze through attempting to smoke her cigarette at the table, and watching the cigarette burn on its own, I was more than happy to make the announcement that it was time for bed. This is when she would come to life and say sometimes very sternly, "I want a cigarette."

"Nope, it's time for bed, "I would tell her. There were many times like this, enough times to fill another book, but after I paint a picture of just one incident, you will get a feel for the anger she felt after being told "no." it had her kicking and screaming.

Marjorie hated to hear the word "no." When I told her no to the second cigarette in the middle of the night, she informed me that she intended to tear the whole house apart. Even at less than 90 pounds, she had capabilities.

The tirades would usually start with her berating me. One day she reached back and pulled the phone receiver off the wall. She yelled into the receiver, "Police, police." At the same time, I was trying to disconnect the phone from the wall.

Minutes later she pulled the curtains off the window, knocked everything off the table and then, while still sitting in her wheelchair, she lifted the table up and got if halfway turned over before I was able to retrieve it.

For those of you who are saying, "Why not just let her have a second cigarette?" I'll tell you why. It wasn't that I was opposed to the smoking, not even in the middle of the night. I decided I was even willing to lose sleep so she could smoke.

However, about the fifth or sixth time she dropped the lit cigarette in her lap, on the floor, or on the table, because she was too weak to hold on to it, I was done with the overnight cigarette fiasco.

"It's time for bed," I said, ignoring the constant pleading for the second cigarette. On the way back to her hospital bed, which was only about 15 feet from the kitchen or cigarette room, she tried to throw herself out of the wheelchair. "You are going to let me smoke another cigarette or I'll make you sorry you didn't," she would say.

I would always manage to get Marjorie back into bed but from the room where I was sleeping, I could hear her calling for help again and again. "Help, help, somebody help me." Of course, I couldn't sleep so I went to check on her. When I would get there, she might be trying to get out of bed. One time I found her wedged between the wall and the bars on the hospital bed that had been put on to keep her from trying to crawl out.

Marjorie, what have you done? Now I have to rescue her without hurting her. It was a lot more complicated than it sounds. But the whole time I was trying to free her, she was saying, "Are you going to let me smoke a cigarette?"

"You can't smoke in this position," I told her as I continued to try to free her small frame from between the wall and the bedrail. I managed to get her back into the bed while she was still cursing and screaming at me about another cigarette. There were many times like this.

Even when I tried to redirect her by showing an interest in getting to know her better, (and at the same time hoping to take her mind off the cigarettes), she would snap, "Don't you ask me another question about my life! I don't want you to know anything about me and I don't want to know anything about you."

Did I say she had five other caregivers (before me) who refused to work with her. The family saw moods that were even worse, so they had understandably given up the idea of any social visits. They made sure she had what she needed, gave me a little pity and waved goodbye when they drove off. I refused to give up on her.

My supervisor called me several times to ask if I needed her to relieve me so I could take a walk or go to the nearby coffee shop for a break, but I'd just say, "I'm okay."

I understood that Marjorie was very angry about her impending death and I knew that eventually she would move into acceptance. I wouldn't say it was easy for me but because "end of life" matters, I was unwilling to leave her with someone who didn't understand.

Furthermore, as a foster parent for teens and a person who has a history of working with people who are mentally ill and emotionally disturbed, a juvenile detention volunteer and a criminal justice professional, I have been berated and cursed out by the best of them.

Someone is probably thinking: "If she was in hospice, why didn't someone order something to help her calm down?" The answer to that question is, of course they did. It didn't help. She was angry and nothing would change that. Not a calming prescription during the day, or a pill to help her sleep at night. She had a constitution that was so full of anger over her impending death that nothing was going to calm her.

As much as it might seem hard to believe, my client did not die in the anger stage. Twenty-four hours before she died, she did move into the acceptance stage. The night before she died, we were at the kitchen table. She was smoking, of course.

But something was different. She was very calm and seemed to want to talk (for the first time) about her feelings about death. I asked her if she was afraid. I knew she had been afraid during the previous weeks I had spent with her, but she had finally come to terms with it.

That night, we talked about her life, her family, her friends, her best friend, her jobs and even the reason she chose not to ever marry. I was on cloud nine. After our talk, she got back to bed without incident. The next day she asked me to call her sister. "I think it's time and I'm ready," she said.

By the time her sister arrived, she was weaker but calm and comfortable. Before her sister moved in close to talk to her, I took her hand and I said, "Marjorie, I had a great time getting to know you last night. We've never had an opportunity to share like that and it meant the world to me."

She said, "I guess now I can call you friend." I walked into her kitchen and cried. Marjorie died later that day.

The Married Couple

Another one of my end-of-life hospice experiences was a blessing to me right from the start. I worked with a couple who had been married for 64 years and who had been together for 68 years. She was 94 years old, and he was 96. They were two of the sweetest people in this whole wide world. He was dying of prostate cancer. The best part is the two of them were visibly still madly in love.

They had spent all their lives focusing on one another because they never had kids. One time I asked if they had ever had pets and the wife told me that they travelled a lot together and wouldn't have known what to do with a pet every time they took off.

When I met this couple, the wife was still very independent and, for the most part, did everything for herself and her husband. She was reluctant to accept help initially, so I took a back seat and let her care for her husband the same way she had cared for him for 64 years. When I noticed that she was getting tired, I would step in and offer a helping hand.

I was holding his hand with her when he died. She died two months later, which is what she said she wanted when he took his last breath. "I want to go too," she said. "I cannot live without him."

People who are dying teach us many things. They teach us that we should never let things go unsaid. They teach us that, in the end, the small things really are small things. They remind us that it's important to live life to the fullest—and in the words of Anna Quindlen, they [should] teach us to…

"Consider the lilies of the field. Look at the fuzz on a baby's ear. Read in the backyard with the sun on your face. Learn to be happy. And think of life as a terminal illness because if you do you will live it with joy and passion as it ought to be."

AFTERWORD

When Oprah Winfrey, on her popular television show Super Soul Sunday, asked Tracy Morgan what he thought was the reason for so much racism in our country, he answered with one word: "Pride." Pride, as defined in the dictionary is a "high or inordinate opinion of one's own dignity, importance, merit, or superiority."

Morgan makes a very good point. We look down on others not only because we are prideful and feel superior. We also do it because looking down on others makes us feel better about ourselves. Let me add another caveat. We look down on people or are intolerant of their differences because of our own low self-esteem and low self-worth.

Steve Harvey recently told a young lady (who said people put her down all the time), that people who put you down and call you names do that because they feel the same way about themselves. He went on to say, and I'm paraphrasing, that people who are not in good positions themselves are not in a position to build others up.

T.D. Jakes brings it on home with his turtle-giraffe story. He says, you can't get a turtle to see a giraffe's perspective. He also said that when the turtle is so close to the ground, he will never see the expanse of the life that the giraffe has been blessed to see.

If you're the giraffe, there is a way to help the turtle understand your perspective. You can allow the turtle into your realm by being open and communicative. You can expose the turtle to your world by exposing him/her to your experiences.

If we are to love the untouchables, welcome the stranger, and love one another as God so loved the world, we must broaden our horizons, (regardless of whether we're the turtle or the giraffe) and as a result we will broaden the horizons of others.

We must reach out to those people who don't look like us, think like us, worship like us, sing praises like us, have freedom like us or love in the same way we do.

We must educate and expose ourselves to the differences in others. In the words of one of Diana Ross's famous songs, "Reach out and touch somebody's hand, make this world a better place if you can." This brings President Obama back to mind. He alludes that we can't accomplish this [song] with clenched fists.

God loves the African American, white people, Asians, Arabs, Hispanics, Indians and every other nationality that is not our own. God loves the disabled individual, people in the LGBTQ community, the Jewish community, the Muslim community, the unchurched, members of the Catholic Church, the Baptist Church, the Lutheran Church, the Pentecostal Church, the Covenant Church, and every other church that is not our own.

God loves those who are justice involved, the substance user, individuals who are homeless and those who are HIV positive. He loves the foster child, the pregnant teen, the motherless, the fatherless, and He loves members of white nationalist groups.

And further, if we are shining His "light of love," that light will reach out and touch "ALL lives [that] matter" because unlike people, light does not discriminate, it just shines.

"Darkness cannot drive out darkness; only light can do that. Hate cannot drive out hate; only LOVE can do that."
-Dr. Martin Luther King Jr.

EPILOGUE

Loving God,
Open our hearts to those most in need:
The unemployed parent worried about feeding his or her children.
The woman who is underpaid, harassed or abused.
The Black man or woman who fear for their lives.
The immigrant at the border, longing for safety.
The homeless person looking for a meal.
The LGBTQ teen who is bullied.
The unborn child in the womb.
The inmate on death row.
Help us to be a nation where every life is sacred,
all people are loved,
and all are welcome.
Amen.

---Fr. James Martin's benediction from the final night of the Democratic National Convention

Love is patient, love is kind. It does not boast, it is not proud. It does not dishonor others, it is not self-seeking, it is not easily angered, it keeps no record of wrongs. Love does not delight in evil but rejoices with the truth. It always protects, always trusts, always hopes, always perseveres. Love never fails.

1 Corinthians 13:4-7

References

Chapman, Gary, The Love Languages of God; Copyright 2002, 2009, 2018

Your Daddy Kills Animals, PETA; Peta's comic for Kids

Takes Aim at Dads Who Fish; www.peta.org

Bellamy, Francis, Youth's Companion, September 8, 1892

Dorn, Charles, How a Socialist Ended Up Writing the pledge of Allegiance, September 8, 2017.

Southern Poverty Law Center, Teaching Tolerance, "Hidden Bias: A Primer, the Effects of Prejudice and Stereotypes: www.teachingtolerance.org.

Elder, Larry; What's Race Got to Do With It; Why it's time to stop the stupidest argument in America, March 2009.

Nation Rick; What's So Great About an Ethnically Diverse Church? December 28, 2013.

Friedman, Emily; Pastor Cancels Koran Burning: Deal is Denied, September 9, 2010 www.abcnews.com,

Toth, Reid C, Crews, Gordon A, Burton, Catherine E; In the Margins: "Special Populations and American Justice" 2008. Archbishop Timothy Nolan; "To Whom Shall We Go" 2008.

Frontline, The Basic Tenents of Islam, www.pbs.org.

Ruiz, Don Miquel, MD; "The Four Agreements," 1977.

Raven Wolf, Silver; Teen Witch: Wiccan for a New Generation, 1998.

Haley, Alex; The Autobiography of Malcolm X, 1965.

Hate Crime Statistics Program, www.ucr.fbi.org.

Nuckols, Ben; Man Charged in Museum Guard Murder, Washington Post, 2009.

Williamson, Marianne, American Spiritual Teacher, "Our Deepest Fear" quote.

Keating, Susan, "Former Foster Child Devotes His Life to Helping Thousands of Other Kids in Foster Care—One Backpack at a Time" People Magazine, www.people.com.

Estes, Eleanor: "The Hundred Dresses" 1944.

Steinbeck, John: "Of Mice and Men" 1937.

Kriegistein, Maryann, MSW: Awareness, CASA Training Presentation, 1996.

Allison, Jay, Gediman, Dan: "This I Believe II" The Personal Philosophies of Remarkable Men and Women.

Martin, Marilyn, M.D., M.P.H., Saving Our Last Nerve:

The Black Women's Path to Mental Health, 2002.

www.blackcollegiate.com.

www.blackliveschicago.com.

www.willcountypublicdefender.com.

Oliveira, Burke, "Lost in the Shuffle: Culture of Homeless Adolescents, 2009.

Kim, MJ; Tajima, EA; Herrenkohl, TI; Huang, B: Early Child Maltreatment, Runaway youths, and Risk of Delinquency and Victimization in Adolescence: A mediational model, 2009.

Whitbeck, Chen, Hoyt, Tyler, Johnson; Article: Journal of the American Academy of Child and Adolescent Psychiatry: Victimization and Posttraumatic Stress Disorder Among Adolescents, 2004

Tyler, Beal; Article: The High-Risk Environment of Homeless Young Adults: Consequences for Physical and Sexual Victimization, 2010.

Green, JM; Ennet, ST; Ringwalt, CL; American Public Health Association Journal: Prevalence and correlates of survival sex among runaway and homeless youth, 2009.

BehaveNet Clinical Capsule: Post Traumatic Stress Disorder Handout.

Yoder, KA; Hoyt, DR; Whitbeck, LB; Article in Journal of Youth and Adolescence, Suicidal behavior among homeless and runaway adolescents, 1998.

Bean, Carl, Archbishop; I Was Born This Way: A Gay Preacher's Journey Through Gospel Music, Disco Stardom and a Ministry in Christ, 2010.

www.civilrights.org.

www.stormfront.com

Ramirez, Hoopes & Quinlin, Defining Racial Profiling in a Post September 11 World, 2003.

Satzewich, Vic; Shaffir, William; Racism versus Professionalism: Claims and Counterclaims about Racial Profiling, 2009.

McWhorter, John; "Losing the Race: Self Sabotage in Black America," 2000.

National Head Start Association, www.nhsa.org

www.nationalpriorities.org

Kinsley, Michael; Slate Magazine.

Wallace, Harvey; Roberson, Cliff; Victimology: Legal,

Psychological and Social Perspectives, 2014.

Weaver, Heather; American Civil Liberties Union,

ACLU, www.foxnews.com.

Racism test. www.quibblo.com.

CPSIA information can be obtained
at www.ICGtesting.com
Printed in the USA
FSHW011840250421
80725FS